From the Illustrated Series™ Team

At Course Technology we believe that technology will transform the way that people teach and learn. We are very excited about bringing you, instructors and students, the most practical and affordable technology-related products available.

► The Development Process

Our development process is unparalleled in the educational publishing industry. Every product we create goes through an exacting process of design, development, review, and testing.

Reviewers give us direction and insight that shape our manuscripts and bring them up to the latest standards. Every manuscript is quality tested. Students whose backgrounds match the intended audience work through every keystroke, carefully checking for clarity and pointing out errors in logic and sequence. Together with our own technical reviewers, these testers help us ensure that everything that carries our name is as error-free and easy to use as possible.

► The Products

We show both how and why technology is critical to solving problems in the classroom and in whatever field you choose to teach or pursue. Our time-tested, step-by-step instructions provide unparalleled clarity. Examples and applications are chosen and crafted to motivate students.

► The Illustrated Series™ Team

The Illustrated Series™ Team is committed to providing you with the most visual introduction to microcomputer applications. No other series of books will get you up to speed faster in today's changing software environment. This book will suit your needs because it was delivered quickly, efficiently, and affordably. In every aspect of business, we rely on a commitment to quality and the use of technology. Each member of the Illustrated Series™ Team contributes to this process. The names of all our team members are listed below.

The Team

Cynthia Anderson	Pam Conrad	Meta Chaya Hirschl	Elizabeth Eisner Reding
Chia-Ling Barker	Mary Therese Cozzola	Jane Hosie-Bounar	Neil Salkind
Donald Barker	Carol Cram	Steven Johnson	Gregory Schultz
Ann Barron	Kim T. M. Crowley	Bill Lisowski	Ann Shaffer
David Beskeen	Catherine DiMassa	Chet Lyskawa	Dan Swanson
Ann Marie Buconjic	Linda Eriksen	Kristine O'Brien	Marie Swanson
Rachel Bunin	Jessica Evans	Tara O'Keefe	Jennifer Thompson
Joan Carey	Lisa Friedrichsen	Harry Phillips	Sasha Vodnik
Patrick Carey	Jeff Goding	Nicole Jones Pinard	Jan Weingarten
Sheralyn Carroll	Michael Halvorson	Katherine T. Pinard	Christie Williams
Brad Conlin	Jamie Harper	Kevin Proot	Janet Wilson

Preface

►IV

Welcome to *Microsoft Excel 97 – Illustrated Brief Edition*! This book in our highly visual new design offers new users a hands-on introduction to Microsoft Excel 97 and also serves as an excellent reference for future use. If you would like additional coverage of Microsoft Excel 97, we also offer *Microsoft Excel 97 – Illustrated Standard Edition*, a logical continuation of Brief Edition.

► Organization and Coverage

This text contains four units that cover basic Excel skills. In these units students learn how to design, create, edit, and enhance Excel workbooks. They also learn how to create meaningful charts to illustrate their data.

► About this Approach

What makes the Illustrated approach so effective at teaching software skills? It's quite simple. Each skill is presented on two facing pages, with the step-by-step instructions on the left page, and large screen illustrations on the right. Students can focus on a single skill without having to turn the page. This unique design makes information extremely accessible and easy to absorb, and provides a great reference for after the course is over. This hands-on approach also makes it ideal for both self-paced or instructor-led classes. The modular structure of the book also allows for great flexibility; you can cover the units in any order you choose.

Each lesson, or "information display," contains the following elements:

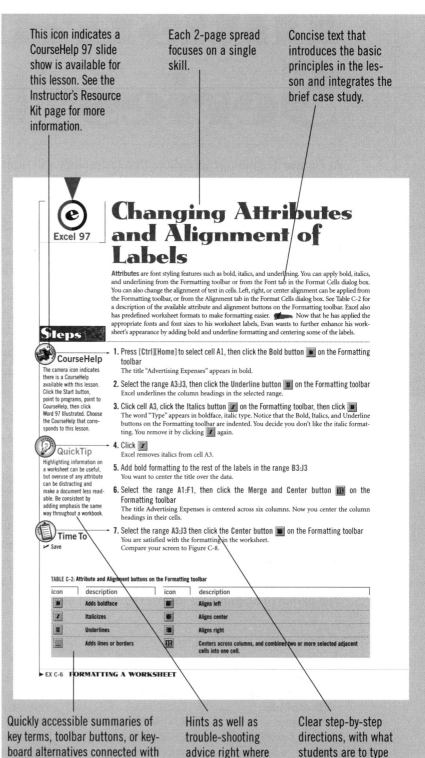

This icon indicates a CourseHelp 97 slide show is available for this lesson. See the Instructor's Resource Kit page for more information.

Each 2-page spread focuses on a single skill.

Concise text that introduces the basic principles in the lesson and integrates the brief case study.

Quickly accessible summaries of key terms, toolbar buttons, or keyboard alternatives connected with the lesson material. Students can refer easily to this information when working on their own projects at a later time.

Hints as well as trouble-shooting advice right where you need it – next to the step itself.

Clear step-by-step directions, with what students are to type in red, explain how to complete the specific task.

Every lesson features large, full-color representations of what the screen should look like as students complete the numbered steps.

The innovative design draws the students' eyes to important areas of the screens.

Brightly colored tabs above the program name indicate which section of the book you are in. Useful for finding your place within the book and for referencing information from the index.

Other Features

The two-page lesson format featured in this book provides the new user with a powerful learning experience. Additionally, this book contains the following features:

▶ Real-World Case

The case study used throughout the textbook, a fictitious company called Nomad Ltd is designed to be "real-world" in nature and introduces the kinds of activities that students will encounter when working with Microsoft Excel. With a real-world case, the process of solving problems will be more meaningful to students.

▶ End of Unit Material

Each unit concludes with a Concepts Review that tests students' understanding of what they learned in the unit. A Skills Review follows the Concepts Review and provides students with additional hands-on practice of the skills they learned in the unit. The Skills Review is followed by Independent Challenges, which pose case problems for students to solve. At least one Independent Challenge in each unit asks students to use the World Wide Web to solve the problem as indicated by a WebWork icon. The Visual Workshops that follow the Independent Challenges help students to develop critical thinking skills. Students are shown completed documents and are asked to recreate them from scratch.

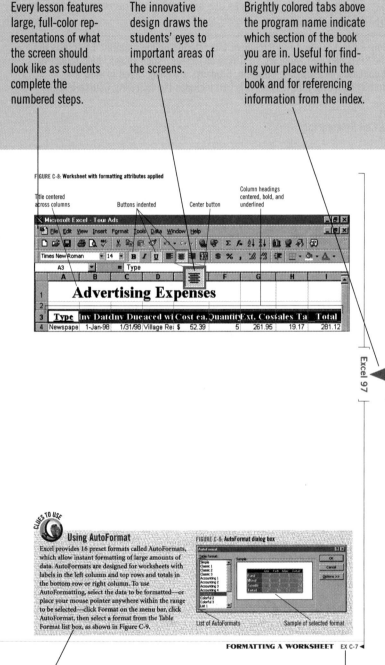

FIGURE C-8: Worksheet with formatting attributes applied

Title centered across columns · Buttons indented · Center button · Column headings centered, bold, and underlined

Advertising Expenses

Excel 97

Using AutoFormat

Excel provides 16 preset formats called AutoFormats, which allow instant formatting of large amounts of data. AutoFormats are designed for worksheets with labels in the left column and top rows and totals in the bottom row or right column. To use AutoFormatting, select the data to be formatted—or place your mouse pointer anywhere within the range to be selected—click Format on the menu bar, click AutoFormat, then select a format from the Table Format list box, as shown in Figure C-9.

FIGURE C-9: AutoFormat dialog box

List of AutoFormats · Sample of selected format

FORMATTING A WORKSHEET EX C-7

Clues to Use Boxes provide concise information that either expands on the major lesson skill or describes an independent task that in some way relates to the major lesson skill.

The page numbers are designed like a road map. EX indicates the Excel section, C indicates the third unit, and 7 indicates the page within the unit. This map allows for the greatest flexibility in content — each unit stands completely on its own.

Instructor's Resource Kit

The Instructor's Resource Kit is Course Technology's way of putting the resources and information needed to teach and learn effectively into your hands. With an integrated array of teaching and learning tools that offer you and your students a broad range of instructional options, we believe this kit represents the highest quality and most cutting edge resources available to instructors today. Many of these resources are available online www.course.com. The resources available with this book are:

CourseHelp 97 CourseHelp 97 is a student reinforcement tool offering online annotated tutorials that are accessible directly from the Start menu in Windows 95. These on-screen "slide shows" help students understand the most difficult concepts in a specific program. Students are encouraged to view a CourseHelp 97 slide show before completing that lesson. This text includes the following CourseHelp 97 side shows:
- Moving and Copying Text
- Relative versus Absolute Cell Referencing
- Choosing a Chart Type

Adopters of this text are granted the right to post the CourseHelp 97 files on any standalone computer or network.

Course Test Manager Designed by Course Technology, this cutting edge Windows-based testing software helps instructors design and administer tests and pre-tests. This full-featured program also has an online testing component that allows students to take tests at the computer and have their exams automatically graded.

Course Online Faculty Companion This new World Wide Web site offers Course Technology customers a password-protected Faculty Lounge where you can find everything you need to prepare for class. These periodically updated items include lesson plans, graphic files for the figures in the text, additional problems, updates and revisions to the text, links to other Web sites, and access to Student Disk files. This new site is an ongoing project and will continue to evolve throughout the semester. Contact your Customer Service Representative for the site address and password.

Course Online Student Companion This book features its own Online Companion where students can go to access Web sites that will help them complete the WebWork Independent Challenges. This page also contains links to other Course Technology student pages where students can find task references for each of the Microsoft Office 97 programs, a graphical glossary of terms found in the text, an archive of meaningful templates, software, hot tips, and Web links to other sites that contain pertinent information. These new sites are also ongoing projects and will continue to evolve throughout the semester.

Student Files To use this book students must have the Student Files. See the inside front or inside back cover for more information on the Student Files. Adopters of this text are granted the right to post the Student Files on any stand-alone computer or network.

Instructor's Manual This is quality assurance tested and includes:
- Solutions to all lessons and end-of-unit material
- Unit notes with teaching tips from the author
- Extra Independent Challenges
- Transparency Masters of key concepts
- Student Files
- CourseHelp 97

The Illustrated Family of Products

This book that you are holding fits in the Illustrated Series -- one series of three in the Illustrated family of products. The other two series are the Illustrated Projects Series and the Illustrated Interactive Series. The Illustrated Projects Series is a supplemental series designed to reinforce the skills learned in any skills-based book through the creation of meaningful and engaging projects. The Illustrated Interactive Series is a line of computer-based training multimedia products that offer the novice user a quick and interactive learning experience. All three series are committed to providing you with the most visual and enriching instructional materials.

Contents

Excel 97

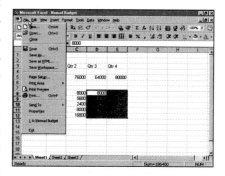

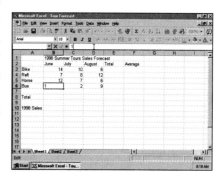

Contents

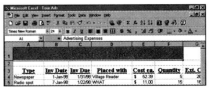

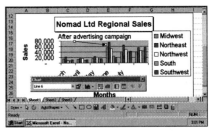

Getting
Started with Excel 97

Objectives

- ► **Define spreadsheet software**
- ► **Start Excel 97**
- ► **View the Excel window**
- ► **Open and save an existing workbook**
- ► **Enter labels and values**
- ► **Preview and print a worksheet**
- ► **Get Help**
- ► **Close a workbook and exit Excel**

In this unit, you will learn how to start Excel and recognize and use different elements of the Excel window and menus. You will also learn how to open existing files, enter data in a worksheet, and use the extensive online Help system. ✎ Evan Brillstein works in the Accounting Department at Nomad Ltd, an outdoor sporting gear and adventure travel company. Evan will use Excel to complete a worksheet that summarizes budget information and create a workbook to track tour sales.

Defining Spreadsheet Software

Excel is an electronic spreadsheet that runs on Windows computers. An **electronic spreadsheet** uses a computer to perform numeric calculations rapidly and accurately. See Table A-1 for common ways spreadsheets are used in business. An electronic spreadsheet is also referred to as a **worksheet**, which is the document that you produce when you use Excel. A worksheet created with Excel allows Evan to work quickly and efficiently, and to update the results accurately and easily. He will be able to produce more professional-looking documents with Excel. Figure A-1 shows a budget worksheet that Evan and his manager created using pencil and paper. Figure A-2 shows the same worksheet that they can create using Excel.

Details

Excel is better than the paper system for the following reasons:

Enter data quickly and accurately

With Excel, Evan can enter information faster and more accurately than he could using the pencil-and-paper method. For example, in the Nomad Ltd. Budget, Evan can use Excel to calculate Total Expenses and Net Income for each quarter by simply supplying the data and formulas, and Excel calculates the rest.

Recalculate easily

Fixing errors using Excel is easy, and any results based on a changed entry are recalculated automatically. If Evan receives updated Expense figures for Qtr 4, he can simply enter the new numbers and Excel will recalculate the spreadsheet.

Perform what-if analysis

One of the most powerful decision-making features of Excel is the ability to change data and then quickly recalculate changed results. Anytime you use a worksheet to answer the question "what if," you are performing a what-if analysis. For instance, if the advertising budget for May were increased to $3,000, Evan could enter the new figure into the spreadsheet and immediately find out the impact on the overall budget.

Change the appearance of information

Excel provides powerful features for enhancing a spreadsheet so that information is visually appealing and easy to understand. Evan can use boldface type and shading to add emphasis to key data in the worksheet.

Create charts

Excel makes it easy to create charts based on information in a worksheet. With Excel, charts are automatically updated as data changes. The worksheet in Figure A-2 includes a pie chart that graphically shows the distribution of Nomad Ltd. expenses for the first quarter.

Share information with other users

Because everyone at Nomad is now using Microsoft Office, it's easy for Evan to share information with his colleagues. If Evan wants to use the data from someone else's worksheet, he accesses their files through the network or by disk. For example, Evan can complete the budget for Nomad Ltd. that his manager started creating in Excel.

Create new worksheets from existing ones quickly

It's easy for Evan to take an existing Excel worksheet and quickly modify it to create a new one. When Evan is ready to create next year's budget, he can use this budget as a starting point.

FIGURE A-1: Traditional paper worksheet

<table>
<tr><th></th><th colspan="5">Nomad Ltd</th></tr>
<tr><th></th><th>Qtr 1</th><th>Qtr 2</th><th>Qtr 3</th><th>Qtr 4</th><th>Total</th></tr>
<tr><td>Net Sales</td><td>48,000</td><td>76,000</td><td>64,000</td><td>80,000</td><td>268,000</td></tr>
<tr><td>Expenses:</td><td></td><td></td><td></td><td></td><td></td></tr>
<tr><td>Salary</td><td>8,000</td><td>8,000</td><td>8,000</td><td>8,000</td><td>32,000</td></tr>
<tr><td>Interest</td><td>4,800</td><td>5,600</td><td>6,400</td><td>7,200</td><td>24,000</td></tr>
<tr><td>Rent</td><td>2,400</td><td>2,400</td><td>2,400</td><td>2,400</td><td>9,600</td></tr>
<tr><td>Ads</td><td>3,600</td><td>8,000</td><td>16,000</td><td>20,000</td><td>47,600</td></tr>
<tr><td>COG</td><td>16,000</td><td>16,800</td><td>20,000</td><td>20,400</td><td>73,200</td></tr>
<tr><td>Total Exp</td><td>34,800</td><td>40,800</td><td>52,800</td><td>58,000</td><td>186,400</td></tr>
<tr><td>Net Income</td><td>13,200</td><td>35,200</td><td>11,200</td><td>22,000</td><td>81,600</td></tr>
</table>

FIGURE A-2: Excel worksheet

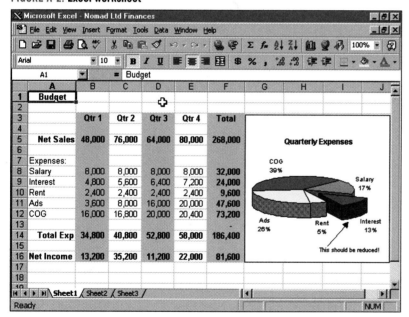

TABLE A-1: Common business spreadsheet uses

use	solution
Maintenance of values	Calculation of figures
Visual representation of values	Chart based on worksheet figures
Create consecutively numbered pages using multiple workbook sheets	Report containing workbook sheets
Organize data	Sort data in ascending or descending order
Analyze data	PivotTable or AutoFilter to create data summaries and short-lists
Create what-if data situations	Scenarios containing data outcomes using variable values

Excel 97

Starting Excel 97

To start Excel, you use the Start Button on the taskbar. Click Programs, then click the Microsoft Excel program icon. A slightly different procedure might be required for computers on a network and those that use utility programs to enhance Windows 95. If you need assistance, ask your instructor or technical support person for help. ➤ Evan's manager has started creating the Nomad Ltd budget and has asked Evan to finish it. He begins by starting Excel now.

1. **Point to the Start button** ⊞Start **on the taskbar**
   The Start button is on the left side of the taskbar and is used to start, or launch, programs on your computer.

2. **Click** ⊞Start
   Microsoft Excel is located in the Programs group—located at the top of the Start menu, as shown in Figure A-3.

Trouble?

If you don't see the Microsoft Excel icon, look for a program group called Microsoft Office.

3. **Point to Programs on the Start menu**
   All the programs, or applications, found on your computer can be found in this area of the Start menu.
   You can see the Microsoft Excel icon and other Microsoft programs, as shown in Figure A-4. Your desktop might look different depending on the programs installed on your computer.

Trouble?

If the Office Assistant appears on your screen, simply choose to start Excel.

4. **Click the Microsoft Excel program icon on the Program menu**
   Excel opens and a blank worksheet appears. In the next lesson, you will familiarize yourself with the elements of the Excel worksheet window.

FIGURE A-3: **Start menu**

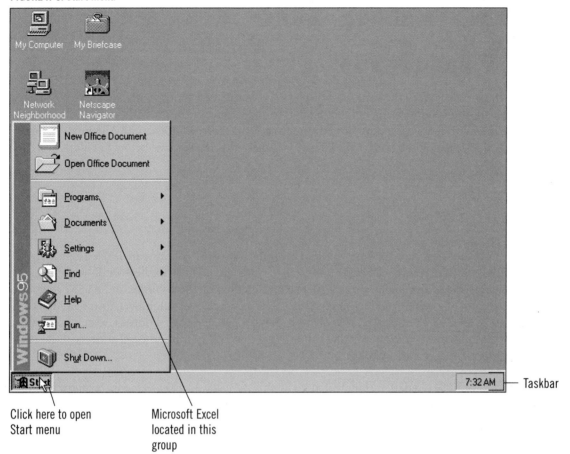

Click here to open
Start menu

Microsoft Excel
located in this
group

Taskbar

FIGURE A-4: **Programs available on your computer**

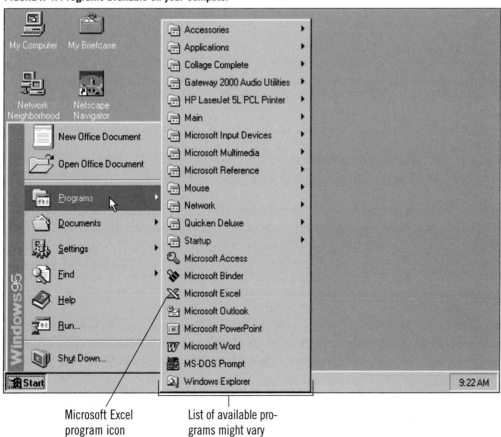

Microsoft Excel
program icon

List of available pro-
grams might vary

Viewing the Excel Window

When you start Excel, the computer displays the **worksheet window**, the area where you enter data, and the window elements that enable you to create and work with worksheets. Evan needs to familiarize himself with the Excel worksheet window and its elements before he starts working with the budget worksheet. Compare the descriptions below to Figure A-5.

The **worksheet window** contains a grid of columns and rows. Columns are labeled alphabetically (A, B, C, etc.) and rows are labeled numerically (1, 2, 3, etc.). The worksheet window displays only a tiny fraction of the whole worksheet, which has a total of 256 columns and 65,533 rows. The intersection of a column and a row is a **cell**. Cells can contain text, numbers, formulas, or a combination of all three. Every cell has its own unique location or **cell address**, which is identified by the coordinates of the intersecting column and row. For example, the cell address of the cell in the upper-left corner of a worksheet is A1.

Trouble?

If your worksheet does not fill the screen as shown in Figure A-5, click the Maximize button in the worksheet window.

The **cell pointer** is a dark rectangle that highlights the cell you are working in, or the **active cell**. In Figure A-5, the cell pointer is located at A1, so A1 is the active cell. To make another cell active, click any other cell or press the arrow keys on your keyboard to move the cell pointer to another cell in the worksheet.

The **title bar** displays the program name (Microsoft Excel) and the filename of the open worksheet (in this case, Book1). The title bar also contains a control menu box, a Close button, and resizing buttons.

The **menu bar** contains menus from which you choose Excel commands. As with all Windows programs, you can choose a menu command by clicking it with the mouse or by pressing [Alt] plus the underlined letter in the menu name, referred to as the command's **shortcut key**.

The **name box** displays the active cell address. In Figure A-5, "A1" appears in the name box, indicating that A1 is the active cell.

The **formula bar** allows you to enter or edit data in the worksheet.

The **toolbars** contain buttons for the most frequently used Excel commands. The **Standard** toolbar is located just below the menu bar and contains buttons corresponding to the most frequently used Excel features. The **Formatting** toolbar contains buttons for the most common commands used for improving the worksheet's appearance. To choose a button, simply click it with the left mouse button. The face of any button has a graphic representation of its function; for instance, the Printing button has a printer on its face.

Sheet tabs below the worksheet grid enable you to keep your work in collections called **workbooks**. Each workbook contains 3 worksheets by default and can contain a maximum of 255 sheets. Sheet tabs can be given meaningful names. **Sheet tab scrolling buttons** help you move from one sheet to another.

The **status bar** is located at the bottom of the Excel window. The left side of the status bar provides a brief description of the active command or task in progress. The right side of the status bar shows the status of important keys, such as the Caps Lock key and the Num Lock key.

FIGURE A-5: **Excel worksheet window elements**

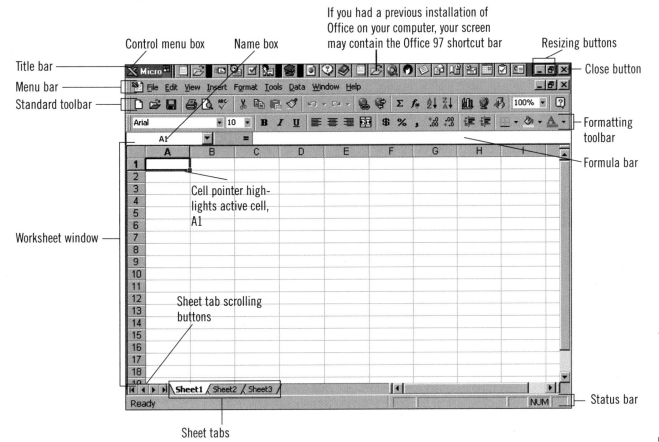

Control menu box   Name box

If you had a previous installation of
Office on your computer, your screen
may contain the Office 97 shortcut bar

Resizing buttons

Title bar

Menu bar

Standard toolbar

Close button

Formatting toolbar

Formula bar

Cell pointer high-
lights active cell,
A1

Worksheet window

Sheet tab scrolling
buttons

Status bar

Sheet tabs

GETTING STARTED WITH EXCEL 97   EX A-7 ◄

Excel 97

Opening and Saving an Existing Workbook

Sometimes it's more efficient to create a new worksheet by modifying one that already exists. This saves you from having to retype information. Throughout this book, you will be instructed to open a file from your Student Disk, use the Save As command to create a copy of the file with a new name, and then modify the new file by following the lesson steps. Saving the files with new names keeps your original Student Disk files intact in case you have to start the lesson over again or you wish to repeat an exercise. ◄▬ Evan's manager has asked Evan to enter information into the Nomad Ltd budget. Follow along as Evan opens the Budget workbook, then uses the Save As command to create a copy with a new name.

**Steps**

Trouble?

If necessary, you can download your student files from our Web Site at http:\\course.com.

1. Insert your Student Disk in the appropriate disk drive

2. Click the **Open button** 📂 on the Standard toolbar
The Open dialog box opens. See Figure A-6.

3. Click the **Look in list arrow**
A list of the available drives appears. Locate the drive that contains your Student Disk.

4. Click the drive that contains your Student Disk
A list of the files on your Student Disk appears in the Look in list box, with the default filename placeholder in the File name text box already selected.

5. In the File name list box click **XL A-1**, then click **Open**
The file XL A-1 opens. You could also double-click the filename in the File name list box to open the file. To create and save a copy of this file with a new name, you use the Save As command.

6. Click **File** on the menu bar, then click **Save As**
The Save As dialog box opens.

QuickTip

You can also click 💾 on the Standard Toolbar or use the shortcut key [Ctrl][S] to save.

7. Make sure the Save in list box displays the drive containing your Student Disk
You should save all your files to your Student Disk, unless instructed otherwise.

8. In the File name text box, double-click the current file name to select it (if necessary), then type **Nomad Budget** as shown in Figure A-7.

QuickTip

Use the Save As command to create a new workbook from one that already exists; use the Save command to store any changes on your disk made to an existing file since the last time the file was saved.

9. Click **Save** to save the file and close the Save As dialog box, then click **OK** to close the Summary Info dialog box if necessary
The file XL A-1 closes, and a duplicate file named Nomad Budget opens, as shown in Figure A-8. To save the workbook in the future, you can click File on the menu bar, then click Save, or click the Save button on the Standard toolbar.

FIGURE A-6: Open dialog box

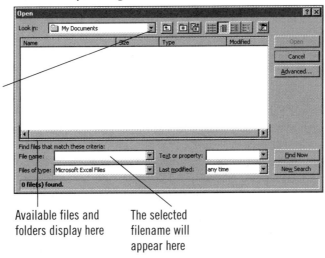

Click to display a
list of available
drives

Available files and
folders display here

The selected
filename will
appear here

FIGURE A-7: Save As dialog box

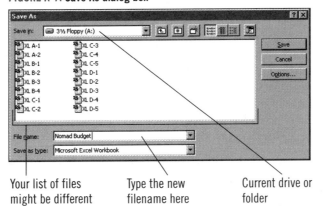

Your list of files
might be different

Type the new
filename here

Current drive or
folder

FIGURE A-8: Nomad Budget workbook

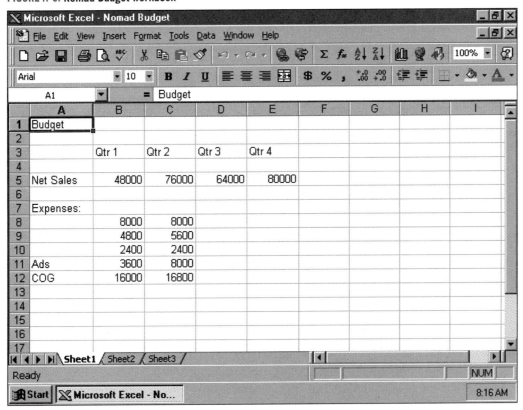

Entering Labels and Values

Labels are used to identify the data in the rows and columns of a worksheet. They are also used to make your worksheet readable and understandable. For these reasons, you should enter all labels in your worksheet first. Labels can contain text and numerical information not used in calculations, such as dates, times, or addresses. Labels are left-aligned by default. **Values**, which include numbers, formulas, and functions, are used in calculations. Excel recognizes an entry as a value when it is a number or begins with one of these symbols: +, -, =, @, #, or $. All values are right-aligned by default. When a cell contains both text and numbers, Excel recognizes the entry as a label. Evan needs to enter labels identifying expense categories, and the values for Qtr 3 and Qtr 4 into the Nomad budget worksheet.

Steps 1 2 3 4

1. **Click cell A8 to make it the active cell**
   Notice that the cell address A8 appears in the name box. You will now enter text for the expenses.

2. **Type Salary, as shown in Figure A-9, then click the Enter button** ☑ **on the formula bar**
   You must click ☑ to confirm your entry. You can also confirm a cell entry by pressing [Enter], pressing [Tab], or by pressing one of the arrow keys on your keyboard. If a label does not fit in a cell, Excel displays the remaining characters in the next cell to the right as long as it is empty. Otherwise, the label is **truncated**, or cut off. The contents of A8, the active cell, display in the formula bar.

3. **Click cell A9, type Interest, then press [Enter] to complete the entry and move the cell pointer to cell A10; type Rent in cell A10, then press [Enter]**
   Now you enter the remaining expense values.

4. **Drag the mouse over cells D8 through E12**
   Two or more selected cells is called a **range**. Since these entries cover multiple columns and rows, you can pre-select the range to make the data entry easier.

5. **Type 8000, then press [Enter]; type 6400 in cell D9, then press [Enter]; type 2400 in cell D10, then press [Enter]; type 16000 in cell D11, then press [Enter]; type 20000 in cell D12, then press [Enter]**
   You have entered all the values in the Qtr 3 column. The cell pointer is now in cell E8. Finish entering the expenses in column E.

6. **Type the remaining values for cells E8 through E12 using Figure A-10 as a guide**

7. **Click the Save button** 🖫 **on the Standard toolbar**
   It is a good idea to save your work often. A good rule of thumb is to save every 15 minutes or so as you modify your worksheet, especially before making significant changes to the worksheet, or before printing.

FIGURE A-9: Worksheet with initial label entered

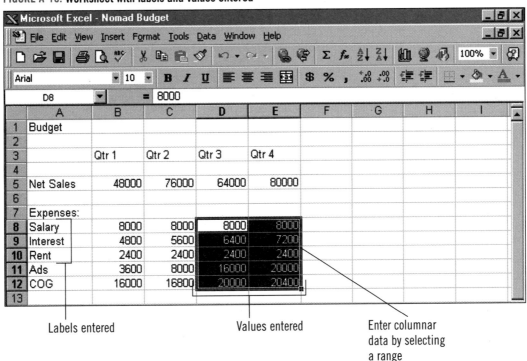

Name box   Cancel button   Enter button

Formula bar

	A	B	C	D	E	F	G	H	I
1	Budget								
2									
3		Qtr 1	Qtr 2	Qtr 3	Qtr 4				
4									
5	Net Sales	48000	76000	64000	80000				
6									
7	Expenses:								
8	Salary	8000	8000						
9		4800	5600						
10		2400	2400						
11	Ads	3600	8000						
12	COG	16000	16800						
13									

FIGURE A-10: Worksheet with labels and values entered

Microsoft Excel - Nomad Budget

D8 = 8000

	A	B	C	D	E	F	G	H	I
1	Budget								
2									
3		Qtr 1	Qtr 2	Qtr 3	Qtr 4				
4									
5	Net Sales	48000	76000	64000	80000				
6									
7	Expenses:								
8	Salary	8000	8000	8000	8000				
9	Interest	4800	5600	6400	7200				
10	Rent	2400	2400	2400	2400				
11	Ads	3600	8000	16000	20000				
12	COG	16000	16800	20000	20400				
13									

Labels entered   Values entered   Enter columnar
                                                data by selecting
                                                a range

CLUES TO USE

Navigating the worksheet

With over a billion cells available to you, it is important to know how to move around, or navigate, the worksheet. You can use the pointer-movement keys ([↑], [↓], [←], [→]) to move a cell or two at a time, or the [Page Up] or [Page Down] to move a screenful at a time. You can also simply use your mouse pointer to click the desired cell. If the desired cell is not visible in the worksheet window, you can use the scroll bars, or the Go To command to move the location into view. To return to the top of the worksheet, cell A1, press [Ctrl][Home].

Excel 97

Previewing and Printing a Worksheet

When a worksheet is completed, you print it to have a paper copy to reference, file, or send to others. You can also print a worksheet that is not complete to review it or work on when you are not at a computer. Before you print a worksheet, you should first save it, as you did at the end of the previous lesson. That way, if anything happens to the file as it is being sent to the printer, you will have a clean copy saved to your disk. Then you should preview it to make sure that it will fit on the page the way you want. When you preview a worksheet, you see a copy of the worksheet exactly as it will appear on paper. Table A-2 provides printing tips. ◄▬▬ Evan is finished entering the labels and values into the Nomad Ltd budget as his manager asked him to. Before he submits it to her for review, he previews it and then prints a copy.

Steps

1. Make sure the printer is on and contains paper

If a file is sent to print and the printer is off, an error message appears. You preview the worksheet to check its overall appearance.

2. Click the Print Preview button on the Standard toolbar

You could also click File on the menu bar, then click Print Preview. A miniature version of the worksheet appears on the screen, as shown in Figure A-11. If there was more than one page, you could click Next and Previous to move between pages. You can also enlarge the image by clicking the Zoom button. After verifying that the preview image is correct, print the worksheet.

3. Click Print

The Print dialog box opens, as shown in Figure A-12.

4. Make sure that the Active Sheet(s) radio button is selected and that 1 appears in the Number of Copies text box

Now you are ready to print the worksheet.

5. Click OK

The Printing dialog box appears while the file is sent to the printer. Note that the dialog box contains a Cancel button that you can use to cancel the print job.

TABLE A-2: Worksheet printing tips

before you print	recommendation
Check the printer	Make sure that the printer is turned on and online, that it has paper, and that there are no error messages or warning signals
Preview the worksheet	Check the formatted image for page breaks, page setup (vertical or horizontal), and overall appearance of the worksheet
Check the printer selection	Use the Printer setup command in the Print dialog box to verify that the correct printer is selected

FIGURE A-11: Print Preview screen

Move to another page   Enlarge the screen image   Print the worksheet   Change print options   Return to worksheet

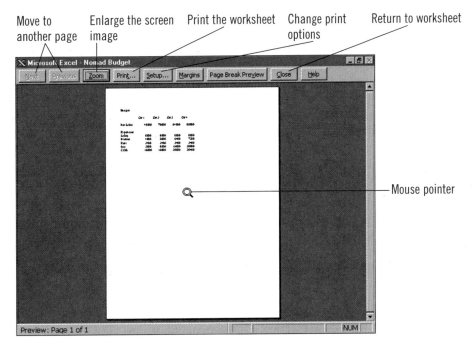

Mouse pointer

Preview: Page 1 of 1

FIGURE A-12: Print dialog box

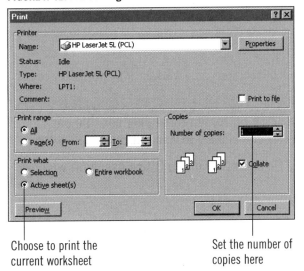

Choose to print the current worksheet

Set the number of copies here

Using Zoom in Print Preview

When you are in the Print Preview window, you can make the image of the page larger by clicking the Zoom button. You can also position the mouse pointer over a specific part of the worksheet page, then click to view that section of the page. While the image is zoomed in, use the scroll bars to view different sections of the page. See Figure A-13.

FIGURE A-13: Enlarging the view using Zoom

Budget				
	Qtr 1	Qtr 2	Qtr 3	Qtr 4
Net Sales	48000	76000	64000	80000
Expenses:				
Salary	8000	8000	8000	8000
Interest	4800	5600	6400	7200
Rent	2400	2400	2400	2400
Ads	3600	8000	16000	20000
COG	16000	16800	20000	20400

Preview: Page 1 of 1

Getting Help

Excel features an extensive online Help system that gives you immediate access to definitions, explanations, and useful tips. The Office Assistant provides this information using a question and answer format. As you are working, the Office Assistant provides tips—indicated by a light bulb you can click—in response to your own working habits. Help appears in a separate balloon-shaped dialog box that you can resize and refer to as you work. You can press the F1 key at any time to get immediate help. Evan knows the manager will want to know the grand total of the expenses in the budget, and he thinks Excel can perform this type of calculation. He decides to use the animated Office Assistant to learn how to see the sum of a range using the AutoCalculate feature, located in the Status bar.

1. Click the Office Assistant button 🔲 on the Standard toolbar

The Office Assistant helps you find information using a question and answer format.

2. Once the Office Assistant is displayed, click its window to activate the query box

You want information on calculating the sum of a range.

3. Type How can I calculate a range?

See Figure A-15. Once you type a question, the Office Assistant can search for relevant topics from the help files in Excel, from which you can choose.

4. Click Search

The Office Assistant displays several topics related to making quick calculations. See Figure A-16.

QuickTip

Information in Help can be printed by clicking the Options button, then clicking Print Topic.

5. Click Quick calculations on a worksheet

The Quick calculations on a worksheet help window opens.

6. Click View the total for a selected range, press [Esc] once you've read the text, then click the Close button on the dialog box title bar

The Help window closes and you return to your worksheet.

QuickTip

You can close the Office Assistant at any time by clicking its Close button.

7. Click the Close button in the Office Assistant window

Changing the Office Assistant

The default Office Assistant is Clippit, but there are eight others from which you can choose. To change the appearance of the Office Assistant, right-click the Office Assistant window, then click Choose Assistant. Click the Gallery tab, click the Back and Next buttons until you find an Assistant you want to use, then click OK. (You may need your Microsoft Office 97 CD-ROM to change Office Assistants.) Each Office Assistant makes its own unique sounds and can be animated by right-clicking its window and clicking Animate! Figure A-16 displays the Office Assistant dialog box.

FIGURE A-14: Office Assistant dialog box

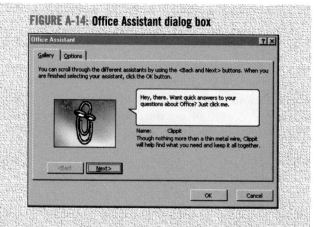

FIGURE A-15: **Office Assistant**

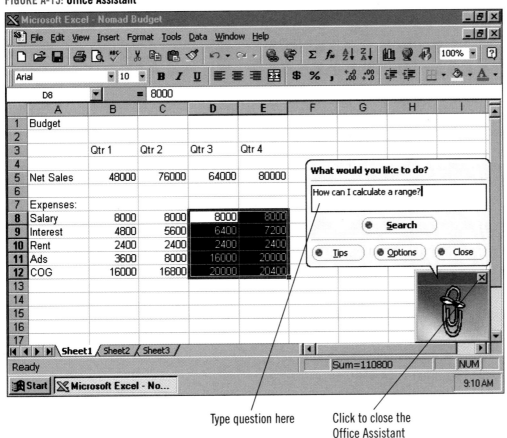

Type question here

Click to close the
Office Assistant

FIGURE A-16: **Relevant Help Assistant topics**

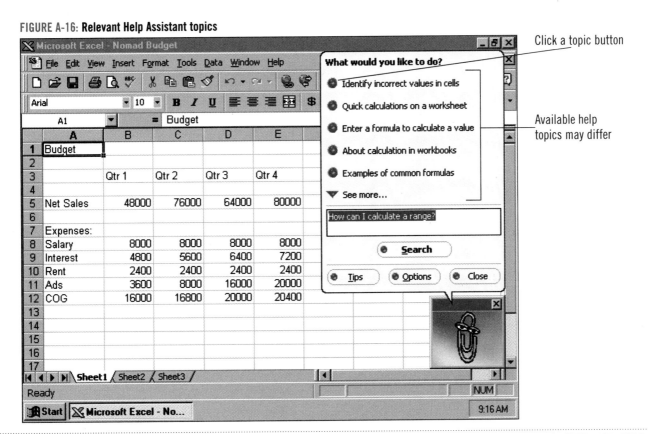

Click a topic button

Available help
topics may differ

Closing a Workbook and Exiting Excel

When you have finished working on a workbook, you need to save the file and close it. Once you have saved a file and are ready to close it, click Close on the File menu. When you have completed all your work in Excel, you need to exit the program. To exit Excel, click Exit on the File menu. ▰▰▰ Evan is done adding the information to the Budget worksheet, and he is ready to pass the printout to his manger to review, so he closes the workbook and then exits Excel.

Steps 1 2 3 4

1. Click **File** on the menu bar

The File menu opens as displayed in Figure A-17.

2. Click **Close**

You could also click the workbook Close button instead of choosing File, then Close. Excel closes the workbook and asks you to save your changes; be sure that you do. A blank worksheet window appears.

Trouble?

To exit Excel and close several files at once, choose Exit from the File menu. Excel will prompt you to save changes to each workbook before exiting.

3. Click **File**, then click **Exit**

You could also click the program Close button to exit the program. Excel closes and computer memory is freed up for other computing tasks.

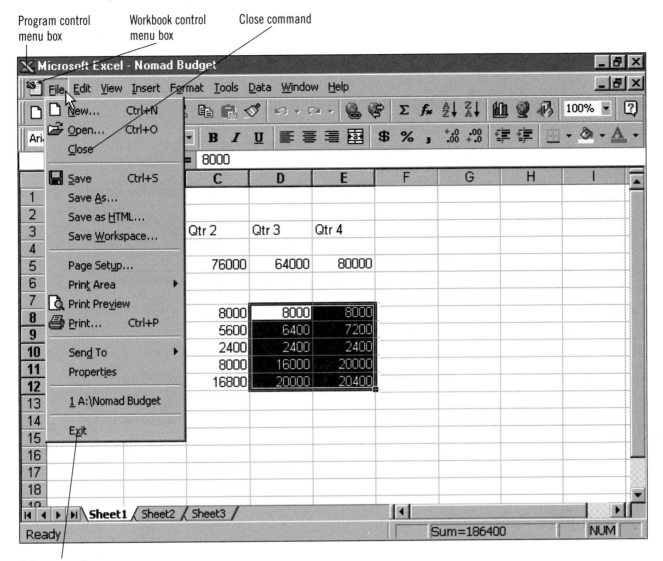

Program control menu box

Workbook control menu box

Close command

Exit command

Excel 97

Practice

► Concepts Review

Label each of the elements of the Excel worksheet window shown in Figure A-18.

FIGURE A-18

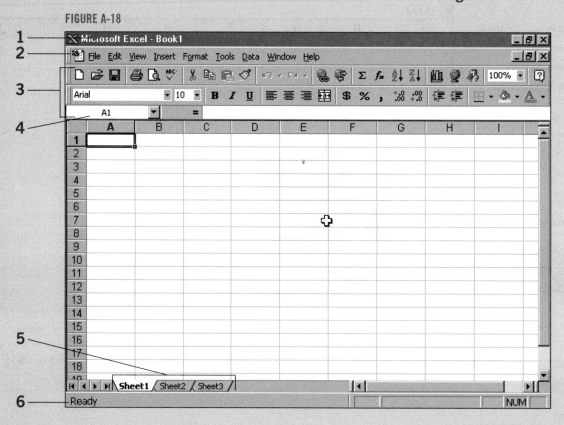

Match each of the terms with the statement that describes its function.

7. Cell pointer e
8. Button c
9. Worksheet window a
10. Name box f
11. Cell b
12. Workbook d

a. Area that contains a grid of columns and rows
b. The intersection of a column and row
c. Graphic symbol that depicts a task or function
d. Collection of worksheets
e. Rectangle that indicates the cell you are currently working in
f. Displays the active cell address

Select the best answer from the list of choices.

13. An electronic spreadsheet can perform all of the following tasks, *except*
  a. Display information visually
  b. Calculate data accurately
  c. Plan worksheet objectives
  d. Recalculate updated information

14. Each of the following is true about labels, *except*
  a. They are left-aligned, by default
  b. They are not used in calculations
  c. They are right-aligned, by default
  d. They can include numerical information

15. Each of the following is true about values, *except*
  a. They can include labels
  b. They are right-aligned, by default
  c. They are used in calculations
  d. They can include formulas

16. What symbol is typed before a number to make the number a label?
  a. "
  b. !
  c. '
  d. ;

17. You can get Excel Help by any of the following ways, *except*
  a. Clicking Help on the menu bar
  b. Pressing [F1]
  c. Clicking the Help button 🔲 on the Standard toolbar
  d. Minimizing the application window

18. Each key(s) can be used to confirm cell entries, *except*
  a. [Enter]
  b. [Tab]
  c. [Esc]
  d. [Shift][Enter]

19. Which button is used to preview a worksheet?
  a. 🔳
  b. 🔳
  c. 🔳
  d. 🔳

20. Which feature is used to enlarge a print preview view?
  a. Magnify
  b. Enlarge
  c. Amplify
  d. Zoom

21. Each of the following is true about the Office Assistant, *except*
  a. It provides tips based on your work habits
  b. It provides help using a question and answer format
  c. You can change the appearance of the Office Assistant
  d. It can complete certain tasks for you

▶ Skills Review

1. Start Excel and identify the elements in the worksheet window.
a. Point to Programs in the Start menu.
b. Click the Microsoft Excel program icon.
c. Try to identify as many elements in the Excel worksheet window as you can without referring to the unit material.

2. Open an existing workbook.
a. Open the workbook XL A-2 by clicking the Open button on the Standard toolbar.
b. Save the workbook as "Country Duds" by clicking File on the menu bar, then clicking Save As.

3. Enter labels and values.
a. Enter labels shown in Figure A-19.
b. Enter values shown in Figure A-19.
c. Save the workbook by clicking the Save button on the Standard toolbar.

FIGURE A-19

	A	B	C	D	E	F	G	H	I
1	Country Duds Clothing Store								
2									
3	Jeans	On-Hand	Cost Each	Sale Price					
4	Button fly	27	9.43						
5	Zipper fly	52	12.09						
6	Heavy wgt	36	15.22						
7	Light wgt	30	11.99						
8	Twill	43	12.72						
9	Khaki	55	9.61						
10									

4. Previewing and printing a worksheet.
a. Click the Print Preview button on the Standard toolbar.
b. Use the Zoom button to see more of your worksheet.
c. Print one copy of the worksheet.
d. Hand in your printout.

5. Get Help.
a. Click the Office Assistant button on the Standard toolbar if the Assistant is not displayed.
b. Ask the Office Assistant for information about changing the Office Assistant character in Excel.
c. Print information offered by the Office Assistant using the Print topic command on the Options menu.
d. Close the Help window.
e. Hand in your printout.

6. Close the workbook and exit Excel.

   a. Click File on the menu bar, then click Close.

   b. If asked if you want to save the worksheet, click No.

   c. If necessary, close any other worksheets you might have opened.

   d. Click File on the menu bar, then click Exit.

▶ Independent Challenges

1. Excel's online Help provides definitions, explanations, procedures, and other helpful information. It also provides examples and demonstrations to show you how Excel features work. Topics include elements such as the active cell, status bar, buttons, and dialog boxes, as well as detailed information about Excel commands and options.

   To complete this independent challenge:

1. Open a new workbook
2. Click the Office Assistant.
3. Type a question that will give you information about opening and saving a worksheet. (Hint: you may have to ask the Office Assistant more than one question.)
4. Print out the information and hand it in.
5. Return to your workbook when you are finished.

2. Spreadsheet software has many uses that can affect the way work is done. Some examples of how Excel can be used are discussed in the beginning of this unit. Use your own personal or business experiences to come up with five examples of how Excel could be used in a business setting.

To complete this independent challenge:

1. Open a new workbook.
2. Think of five business tasks that you could complete more efficiently by using an Excel worksheet.
3. Sketch a sample of each worksheet. See Figure A-20, a sample payroll worksheet.
4. Submit your sketches.

FIGURE A-20

Employee Names	Hours Worked	Hourly Wage	Gross Pay	
Janet Bryce			→	Gross pay=
Anthony Krups			→	Hours worked
Grant Miller			→	times
Barbara Salazar			→	Hourly wage
Total	↓	↓	↓	

3. You are the office manager for Blossoms and Greens, a small greenhouse and garden center. Although the company is just three years old, it is expanding rapidly, and you are continually looking for ways to make your job easier. Last year you began using Excel to manage and maintain data on inventory and sales, which has greatly helped you to track this information accurately and efficiently. However, the job is still overwhelming for just one person. Fortunately, the owner of the company has just approved the hiring of an assistant for you. This person will need to learn how to use Excel. Create a short training document that your new assistant can use as a reference while becoming familiar with Excel.

To complete this independent challenge:

1. Draw a sketch of the Excel worksheet window, and label the key elements, such as toolbars, title bar, formula bar, scroll bars, etc.
2. For each labeled element, write a short description of its use.
3. List the main ways to get Help in Excel. (Hint: use the Office Assistant to learn of all the ways to get help in Excel..)
4. Identify five different ways to use spreadsheets in business.

WEB WORK

4. Data on the World Wide Web is current and informative. It is a useful tool that can be used to gather the most up-to-date information which you can use to make smart buying decisions. Imagine that your supervisor has just told you that due to your great work, she has just found money in the budget to buy you a new computer. You can have whatever you want, but she wants you to justify the expense by creating a spreadsheet using data found on the World Wide Web to support your purchase decision.

To complete this independent challenge:

1. Open a new workbook and save it on your Student Disk as "New Computer Data."
2. Decide which features you want your ideal computer to have, and list these features.
3. Log on to the Internet and use your browser to go to the http://www.course.com. From there, click the link Student On Line Companions, then click the Microsoft Office 97 Professional Edition—Illustrated: A First Course page, then click on the Excel link for Unit A.
4. Use any of the following sites to compile your data: IBM [www.ibm.com], Gateway [www.gw2k.com], Dell [www.dell.com], or any other site you can find with related information.
5. Compile data for the components you want.
6. Make sure all components are listed and totaled. Include any tax and shipping costs the manufacturer charges.
7. Indicate on the worksheet your final purchase decision.
8. Save, print, and hand in your work.

Excel 97

▶ Visual Workshop

Create a worksheet similar to Figure A-21 using the skills you learned in this unit. Save the workbook as "Bea's Boutique" on your Student Disk. Preview, then print the worksheet.

FIGURE A-21

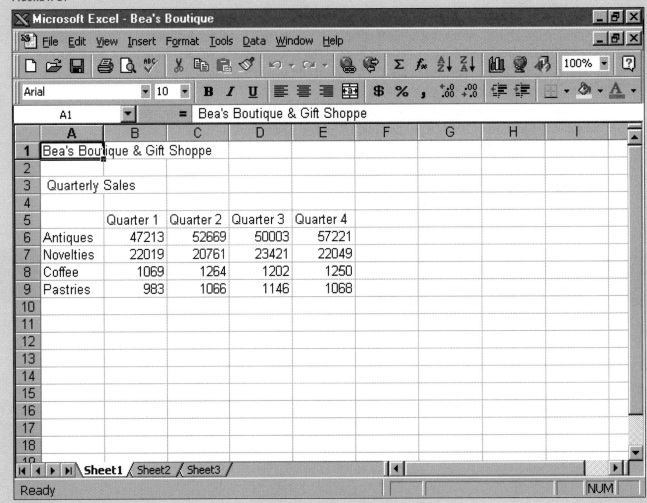

Building
and Editing Worksheets

Objectives

- ► **Plan, design, and create a worksheet**
- ► **Edit cell entries and work with ranges**
- ► **Enter formulas**
- ► **Introduce functions**
- ► **Copy and move cell entries**
- ► **Copy formulas with relative cell references**
- ► **Copy formulas with absolute cell references**
- ► **Name and move a sheet**

You will now plan and build your own worksheets. When you build a worksheet, you enter text, values, and formulas into worksheet cells. Once you create a worksheet, you can save it in a workbook file and then print it. Evan Brillstein has received a request from the Marketing Department for a forecast of this year's summer tour business, and an estimate of the average tour sales for each type of tour. Marketing hopes that the tour business will increase 20% over last year's figures. Evan needs to create a worksheet that summarizes tour sales for last year and a worksheet that forecasts the summer tour sales for this year.

Planning, Designing, and Creating a Worksheet

Before you start entering data into a worksheet, you need to know the purpose and approximate layout of the worksheet. ✎ Evan wants to forecast Nomad's 1998 summer tour sales. The sales goal, already identified by the Marketing Department, is to increase the 1997 summer sales by 20%. Using Figure B-1 and the planning guidelines below, work with Evan as he plans his worksheet.

Details

Determine the purpose of the worksheet and give it a meaningful title
Evan needs to forecast summer tour sales for 1998. Evan titles the worksheet "1998 Summer Tour Sales Forecast."

Determine your worksheet's desired results, sometimes called output
Evan needs to determine what the 1998 sales totals will be if sales increase by 20% over the 1997 sales totals, as well as the average number of tours per type.

Collect all the information, sometimes called input, that will produce the results you want to see
Evan gathers together the sales data for the 1997 summer tour season. The season ran from June through August. The types of tours sold in these months included Bike, Raft, Horse, and Bus.

Determine the calculations, or formulas, necessary to achieve the desired results
First, Evan needs to total the number of tours sold for each month of the 1997 summer season. Then he needs to add these totals together to determine the grand total of summer tour sales. Finally, the 1997 monthly totals and grand total must be multiplied by 1.2 to calculate a 20% increase for the 1998 summer tour season. He'll use the Paste Function to determine the average number of tours per type.

Sketch on paper how you want the worksheet to look; that is, identify where the labels and values will go
Evan decides to put tour types in rows and the months in columns. He enters the tour sales data in his sketch and indicates where the monthly sales totals and the grand total should go. Below the totals, he writes out the formula for determining a 20% increase in sales for 1997. He also includes a label for the location of the tour averages. Evan's sketch of his worksheet is shown in Figure B-1.

Create the worksheet
Evan enters his labels first to establish the structure of his worksheet. He then enters the values, the sales data into his worksheet. These values will be used to calculate the output Evan needs. The worksheet Evan creates is shown in Figure B-2.

1998 Summer Tours Sales Forecast

	June	July	August	Totals	Average
Bike	14	10	6	3 month total	
Raft	7	8	12		
Horse	12	7	6		
Bus	1	2	9		
Totals	June Total	July Total	August Total	Grand Total for 1997	
1998 Sales	Total X 1.2				

FIGURE B-2: Evan's forecasting worksheet

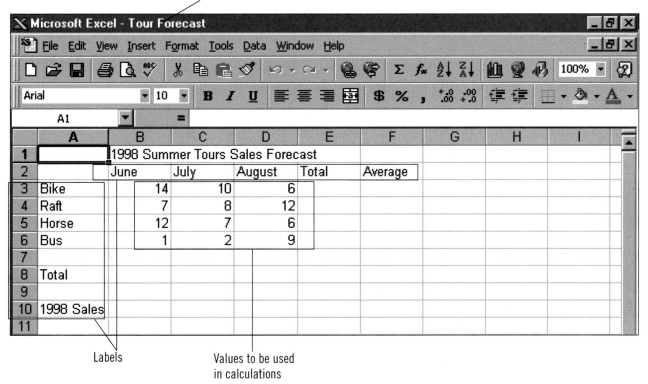

Check title bar for correct title

Labels

Values to be used in calculations

Editing Cell Entries and Working with Ranges

You can change the contents of any cells at any time. To edit the contents of a cell, you first select the cell you want to edit, then click the formula bar, double-click the selected cell, or press [F2]. This puts Excel into Edit mode. To make sure you are in Edit mode, check the **mode indicator** on the far left of the status bar. The mode indicator identifies the current Excel command or operation in progress.   After planning and creating his worksheet, Evan notices that he entered the wrong value for the June bus tours and forgot to include the canoe tours. He fixes the bus tours figure, and he decides to add the canoe sales data to the raft sales figures.

Steps

1. Start Excel, open the workbook XL B-1 from your Student Disk, then save it as **Tour Forecast**

2. Click cell **B6**
   This cell contains June bus tours, which Evan needs to change to 2.

3. Click anywhere in the formula bar
   Excel goes into Edit mode, and the mode indicator displays "Edit." A blinking vertical line, called the **insertion point**, appears in the formula bar, and if you move the mouse pointer to the formula bar, the pointer changes to $\mathbf{I}$ as displayed in Figure B-3.

4. Press [**Backspace**], type **2**, then press [**Enter**] or click the **Enter button** ✓ on the formula bar
   Evan now needs to add "/Canoe" to the Raft label.

5. Click cell **A4** then press [**F2**]
   Excel is in Edit mode again, but this time, the insertion point is in the cell.

6. Type **/Canoe** then press [**Enter**]
   The label changes to Raft/Canoe.

7. Double-click cell **B4**
   Double-clicking a cell also puts Excel into Edit mode with the insertion point in the cell.

8. Press [**Delete**], then type **9**
   See Figure B-4.

9. Click ✓ to confirm the entry

QuickTip

If you make a mistake, you can either click the Cancel button ✗ on the formula bar before accepting the cell entry, or click the Undo button ↺ on the Standard toolbar if you notice the mistake after you have accepted the cell entry. The Undo button allows you to reverse up to 16 previous actions, one at a time.

FIGURE B-3: **Worksheet in Edit mode**

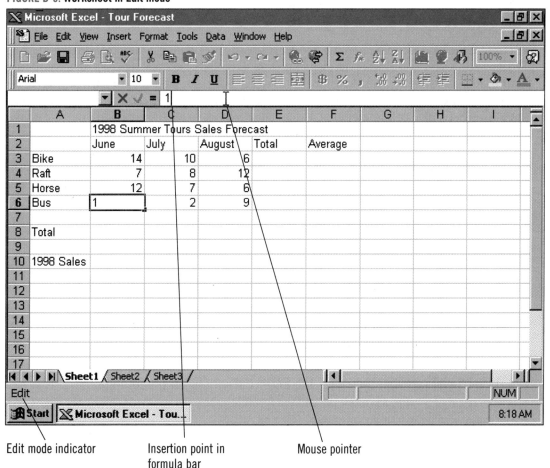

Edit mode indicator   Insertion point in   Mouse pointer
                         formula bar

FIGURE B-4: **Edited worksheet**

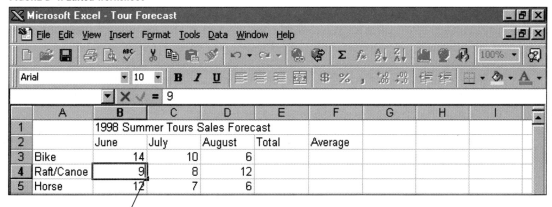

Insertion point in cell

Using range names in a workbook

Any group of cells (two or more) is called a range. To select a range, click the first cell and drag to the last cell you want included in the range. The range address is defined by noting the first and last cells in the range. Give a meaningful name to a range by selecting cells, clicking the name box, and then typing a name. Range names—meaningful English names that Evan uses in this worksheet—are usually easier to remember than cell addresses, they can be used in formulas, and they also help you move around the workbook quickly. Click the name box list arrow, then click the name of the range you want to go to. The cell pointer moves immediately to that range.

Excel 97

Entering Formulas

Formulas are used to perform numeric calculations such as adding, multiplying, and averaging. Formulas in an Excel worksheet start with the formula prefix—the equal sign (=). All formulas use one or more **arithmetic operators** to perform calculations. See Table B-1 for a list of Excel operators. Formulas often contain cell addresses and range names. Using a cell address or range name in a formula is called **cell referencing**. Using cell references keeps your worksheet up-to-date and accurate. If you change a value in a cell, any formula containing that cell reference will be automatically recalculated using the new value. In formulas using more than one arithmetic operator, Excel decides which operation to perform first. ▶ Evan needs to add the monthly tour totals for June, July, and August, and calculate a 20% increase in sales. He can perform these calculations using formulas.

Steps

1. Click cell B8

This is the cell where you want to put the calculation that will total the June sales.

2. Type = (the equal sign)

Placing an equal sign at the beginning of an entry tells Excel that a formula is about to be entered rather than a label or a value. The total June sales is equal to the sum of the values in cells B3, B4, B5, and B6.

Trouble?

If the formula instead of the result appears in the cell after you click ✓, make sure you began the formula with = (the equal sign).

3. Type b3+b4+b5+b6, then click the Enter button ✓ on the formula bar

The result of 37 appears in cell B8, and the formula appears in the formula bar. See Figure B-5. Next, you add the number of tours in July and August.

4. Click cell C8, type =c3+c4+c5+c6, then press [Tab]; in cell D8, type =d3+d4+d5+d6, then press [Enter]

The total tour sales for July, 27, and for August, 33, appear in cells C8 and D8 respectively.

QuickTip

It does not matter if you type the column letter in lower case or upper case when entering formulas. Excel is not case-sensitive—B3 and b3 both refer to the same cell.

5. Click cell B10, type =B8*1.2, then click ✓ on the formula bar

To calculate the 20% increase, you multiply the total by 1.2. This formula calculates the result of multiplying the total monthly tour sales for June, cell B8, by 1.2. The result of 44.4 appears in cell B10.

Now you need to calculate the 20% increase for July and August. You can use the **pointing method**, by which you specify cell references in a formula by selecting the desired cell with your mouse instead of typing its cell reference into the formula.

6. Click cell C10, type =, click cell C8, type *1.2, then press [Tab]

7. Click cell D10, type =, click cell D8, type *1.2, then click ✓

Compare your results with Figure B-6.

TABLE B-1: Excel arithmetic operators

operator	purpose	example
+	Performs addition	=A5+A7
–	Performs subtraction	=A5-10
*	Performs multiplication	=A5*A7
/	Performs division	=A5/A7

FIGURE B-5: Worksheet showing formula and result

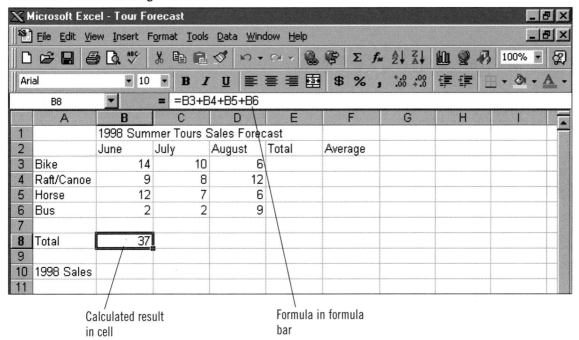

Calculated result
in cell

Formula in formula
bar

FIGURE B-6: Calculated results for 20% increase

Order of precedence in Excel formulas

A formula can include several operations. When you work with formulas that have more than one operator, the order of precedence is very important. If a formula contains two or more operators, such as 4 + .55/4000 * 25, the computer performs the calculations in a particular sequence based on these rules:

Calculated 1st   Calculation of exponents
Calculated 2nd   Multiplication and division, left to right
Calculated 3rd   Addition and subtraction, left to right

In the example 4 + .55/4000 * 25, Excel performs the arithmetic operations by first dividing 4000 into .55, then multiplying the result by 25, then adding 4. You can change the order of calculations by using parentheses. For example, in the formula (4+.55)/4000 * 25, Excel would first add 4 and .55, then divide that amount by 4000, then finally multiply it by 25. Operations inside parentheses are calculated before any other operations.

Introducing Excel Functions

Functions are predefined worksheet formulas that enable you to do complex calculations easily. Like formulas, functions always begin with the formula prefix = (the equal sign). You can enter functions manually, or you can use the Paste Function. ✐ Evan uses the SUM function to calculate the grand totals in his worksheet, and the AVERAGE function to calculate the average number of tours per type.

Steps

1. Click cell **E3**
This is the cell where you want to display the total of all bike tours for June, July, and August. You use the AutoSum button to create the totals. AutoSum sets up the SUM function to add the values in the cells above the cell pointer. If there are no values in the cells above the cell pointer, AutoSum adds the values in the cells to the left of the cell pointer—in this case, the values in cells B3, C3, and D3.

2. Click the **AutoSum button** Σ on the Standard toolbar, then click the **Enter button** ✓ on the formula bar
The formula =SUM(B3:D3) appears in the formula bar. The information inside the parentheses is the **argument**, or the information to be used in calculating a result of the function. An argument can be a value, a range of cells, text, or another function.
The result appears in cell E3. Next, you calculate the total of raft and canoe tours.

3. Click cell **E4**, click Σ, then click ✓
Now you calculate the three-month total of the horse tours.

4. Click cell **E5** then click Σ
AutoSum sets up a function to sum the two values in the cells above the active cell, which is not what you intended. You need to change the argument.

5. Click cell **B5**, then drag to select the range **B5:D5**, then click ✓ to confirm the entry
As you drag, the argument in the SUM function changes to reflect the range being chosen, and a tip box appears telling you the size of the range you are selecting.

6. Enter the SUM function in cells **E6**, **E8**, and **E10**
Make sure you add the values to the left of the active cell, not the values above it. See Figure B-7. Next, you calculate the average number of Bike tours using the Paste Function.

7. Click cell **F3**, then click the **Paste Function button** *f∞* on the Standard toolbar
The Paste Function dialog box opens. See Table B-2 for frequently used functions.
The function needed to calculate averages—named AVERAGE—is included in the Most Recently Used category.

8. Click the function name **AVERAGE** in the Function name list box, click **OK**, then in the AVERAGE dialog box type **B3:D3** in the Number 1 text box, as shown in Figure B-8

Time To
✔ Save

9. Click **OK**, then repeat steps 7, 8 and 9 to calculate the Raft/Canoe (cell **F4**), Horse (cell **F5**), and Bus tours (cell **F6**) averages
The Time To checklist in the left margin contains Steps for routine actions. Everytime you see a Time To checklist, perform the actions listed.

FIGURE B-7: Worksheet with SUM functions entered

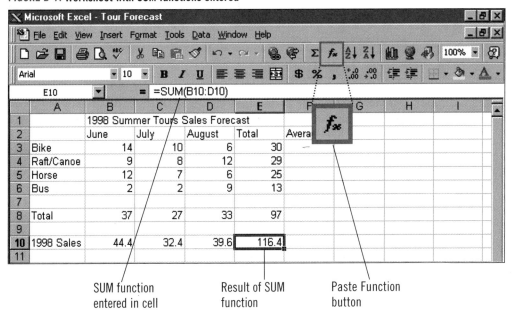

SUM function entered in cell

Result of SUM function

Paste Function button

FIGURE B-8: Using the Paste Function to create a formula

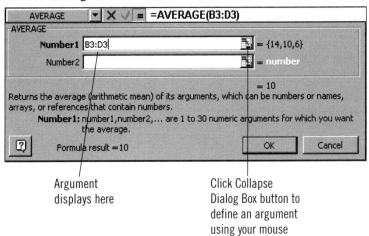

Argument displays here

Click Collapse Dialog Box button to define an argument using your mouse

TABLE B-2: Frequently Used Functions

function	description
SUM(*argument*)	Calculates the sum of the arguments
AVERAGE(*argument*)	Calculates the average of the arguments
MAX(*argument*)	Displays the largest value among the arguments
MIN(*argument*)	Displays the smallest value among the arguments
COUNT(*argument*)	Calculates the number of values in the arguments

Introducing the Paste Function

The Paste Function button f_* is located to the right of the AutoSum button on the Standard toolbar. To use the Paste Function, click f_*. In the Paste Function dialog box, click the category containing the function you want, then click the desired function. The function appears in the formula bar. Click OK to fill in values or cell addresses for the arguments, then click OK.

Excel 97

Copying and Moving Cell Entries

Using the Cut, Copy, and Paste buttons or Excel's drag-and-drop feature, you can copy or move information from one cell or range in your worksheet to another. You can also cut, copy, and paste data from one worksheet to another. ◆▬▬▬ Evan included the 1998 forecast for spring and fall tours sales in his Tour Info workbook. He already entered the spring report in Sheet2 and will finish entering the labels and data for the fall report. Using the Copy and Paste buttons and drag-and-drop, Evan copies information from the spring report to the fall report.

Steps 1234

CourseHelp

The camera icon indicates there is a CourseHelp available with this lesson. Click the Start button, point to programs, point to CourseHelp, then click Excel 97 Illustrated. Choose the CourseHelp that corresponds to this lesson.

1. Click **Sheet 2** of the Tour Forecast workbook
   First, you copy the labels identifying the types of tours from the Spring report to the Fall report.

2. Select the range **A4:A9**, then click the **Copy button** 🖹 on the Standard toolbar

   The selected range (A4:A9) is copied to the **Clipboard**, a temporary storage file that holds all the selected information you copy or cut. The Cut button ✂ removes the selected information from the worksheet and places it on the Clipboard. To copy the contents of the Clipboard to a new location, you click the new cell and then use the Paste command.

3. Click cell **A13**, then click the **Paste button** 🖹 on the Standard toolbar
   The contents of the Clipboard are copied into the range A13:A18. When pasting the contents of the Clipboard into the worksheet, you need to specify only the first cell of the range where you want the copied selection to go. Next, you decide to use drag-and-drop to copy the Total label.

4. Click cell **E3**, then position the pointer on any edge of the cell until the pointer changes to ⬉

5. While the pointer is ⬉, press and hold down **[Ctrl]**
   The pointer changes to ⬉.

Trouble?

When you drag-and-drop into occupied cells, Excel asks if you want to replace the existing cells. Click OK to replace the contents with the cells you are moving.

6. While still pressing **[Ctrl]**, press and hold the left mouse button, then drag the cell contents to cell **E12**
   As you drag, an outline of the cell moves with the pointer, as shown in Figure B-9, and a tip box appears tracking the current position of the item as you move it. When you release the mouse button, the Total label appears in cell E12. You now decide to move the worksheet title over to the left. To use drag-and-drop to move data to a new cell without copying it, do not press [Ctrl] while dragging.

7. Click cell **C1**, then position the mouse on the edge of the cell until it changes to ⬉, then drag the cell contents to **A1**
   You now enter fall sales data into the range B13:D16.

8. Using the information shown in Figure B-10, enter the sales data for the fall tours into the range **B13:D16**
   Compare your worksheet to Figure B-10.

FIGURE B-9: Using drag-and-drop to copy information

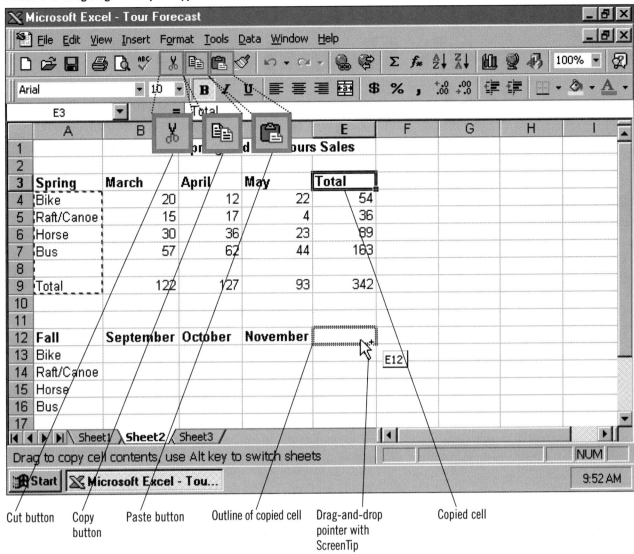

Cut button   Copy   Paste button   Outline of copied cell   Drag-and-drop   Copied cell
              button   pointer with
                                                                  ScreenTip

FIGURE B-10: Worksheet with Fall tours data entered

11					
12	**Fall**	**September**	**October**	**November**	**Total**
13	Bike	17	15	18	
14	Raft/Canoe	21	8	5	
15	Horse	12	21	14	
16	Bus	25	12	18	
17					

◄ ► ► ► \ Sheet1 \ **Sheet2** / Sheet3 /

Ready   Sum=186   NUM

Start   Microsoft Excel - Tou...   9:55 AM

Copying Formulas with Relative Cell References

Copying and moving formulas allows you to reuse formulas you've already created. Copying formulas, rather than retyping them, helps to prevent typing errors. 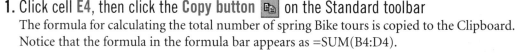 Evan wants to copy from the Spring tours report to the Fall tours report the formulas that total the tours by type and by month. He can use Copy and Paste commands and the Fill right method to copy this information.

CourseHelp

If you have trouble with the concepts in this lesson, be sure to view the CourseHelp entitled Relative versus Absolute Cell Referencing

QuickTip

You can fill cells with sequential months, days of the week, years, and text plus a number (Quarter 1, Quarter 2, . . .) by dragging the fill handle. As you drag the fill handle, the contents of the last filled cell appears in the name box.

QuickTip

Use the Fill Series command on the Edit menu to examine all of Excel's available fill series options.

1. Click cell **E4**, then click the **Copy button** 📋 on the Standard toolbar

The formula for calculating the total number of spring Bike tours is copied to the Clipboard. Notice that the formula in the formula bar appears as =SUM(B4:D4).

2. Click cell **E13**, then click the **Paste button** 📋 on the Standard toolbar

The formula from cell E4 is copied into cell E13, where the new result of 50 appears. Notice in the formula bar that the cell references have changed, so that the range B13:D13 appears in the formula. Formulas in Excel contain **relative cell references**. A relative cell reference tells Excel to copy the formula to a new cell, but to substitute new cell references so that the relationship of the cells to the formula in its new location remains unchanged. In this case, Excel inserted cells D13, C13, and B13, the three cell references immediately to the left of E13.

Notice that the bottom right corner of the active cell contains a small square, called the **fill handle**. Evan uses the fill handle to copy the formula in cell E13 to cells E14, E15, and E16. You can also use the fill handle to copy labels.

3. Position the pointer over the fill handle until it changes to ＋, then drag the fill handle to select the range **E13:E16**

See Figure B-11.

4. Release the mouse button

Once you release the mouse button, the fill handle copies the formula from the active cell (E13) and pastes it into each cell of the selected range. Again, because the formula uses relative cell references, cells E14 through E16 correctly display the totals for Raft and Canoe, Horse, and Bus tours

5. Click cell **B9**, click **Edit** on the menu bar, then click **Copy**

The Copy command on the Edit menu has the same effect as clicking the Copy button 📋 on the Standard toolbar.

6. Click cell **B18**, click **Edit** on the menu bar, then click **Paste**

See Figure B-12. The formula for calculating the September tours sales appears in the formula bar. Now you use the Fill Right command to copy the formula from cell B18 to cells C18, D18, and E18.

7. Select the range **B18:E18**

8. Click **Edit** on the menu bar, point to **Fill**, then click **Right**

The rest of the totals are filled in correctly. Compare your worksheet to Figure B-13.

9. Click the **Save button** 💾 on the Standard toolbar

Your worksheet is now saved.

FIGURE B-11: Selected range using the fill handle

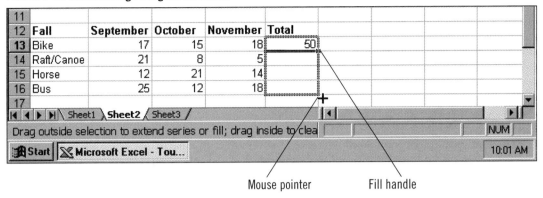

Mouse pointer   Fill handle

FIGURE B-12: Worksheet with copied formula

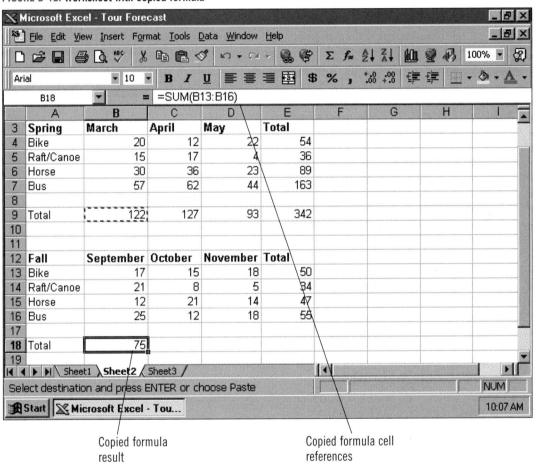

Copied formula   Copied formula cell
result   references

FIGURE B-13: Completed worksheet with all formulas copied

	Fall	September	October	November	Total				
12	Fall	September	October	November	Total				
13	Bike	17	15	18	50				
14	Raft/Canoe	21	8	5	34				
15	Horse	12	21	14	47				
16	Bus	25	12	18	55				
17									
18	Total	75	56	55	186				
19									

Copying Formulas with Absolute Cell References

Sometimes you might want a cell reference to always refer to a particular cell address. In such an instance, you would use an absolute cell reference. An absolute cell reference is a cell reference that always refers to a specific cell address, even if you move the formula to a new location. You identify an absolute reference by placing a dollar sign ($) before the column letter and row number of the address (for example A1). Marketing hopes the tour business will increase by 20% over last year's figures. Evan decides to add a column that calculates a possible increase in the number of spring tours in 1998. He wants to do a what-if analysis and recalculate the spreadsheet several times, changing the percentage that the tours might increase each time.

Steps

1. Click cell **G1**, type **Change**, and then press [→]
You can store the increase factor that will be used in the what-if analysis in cell H1.

2. Type **1.1** in cell **H1**, then press [Enter]
This represents a 10% increase in sales.

3. Click cell **F3**, type **1998?**, then press [Enter]
Now, you create a formula that references a specific address: cell H1.

4. In cell **F4**, type **=E4*H1**, then click the **Enter button** ☑ on the formula bar
The result of 59.4 appears in cell F4. Now use the fill handle to copy the formula in cell F4 to F5:F7.

QuickTip

Before you copy or move a formula, check to see if you need to use an absolute cell reference.

CourseHelp

If you have trouble with the concepts in this lesson, be sure to view the CourseHelp entitled Copying Formulas.

5. Drag the fill handle to select the range **F4:F7**
The resulting values in the range F5:F7 are all zeros. When you look at the formula in cell F5, which is =E5*H2, you realize you need to use an absolute reference to cell H1. You can correct this error by editing cell F4 using [F4], a shortcut key, to change the relative cell reference to an absolute cell reference.

6. Click cell **F4**, press [F2] to change to Edit mode, then press [F4]
When you pressed [F2], the range finder outlined the equations arguments in blue and green. When you pressed [F4], dollar signs appeared, changing the H1 cell reference to an absolute reference. See Figure B-14.

7. Click the ☑ on the formula bar
Now that the formula correctly contains an absolute cell reference, use the fill handle to copy the formula in cell F4 to F5:F7.

8. Drag the fill handle to select the range **F4:F7**
Now you can complete your what-if analysis by changing the value in cell H1 from 1.1 to 1.25 to indicate a 25% increase in sales.

9. Click cell **H1**, type **1.25**, then click the ☑ on the formula bar
The values in the range F4:F7 change. Compare your worksheet to Figure B-15.

FIGURE B-14: Absolute cell reference in cell F4

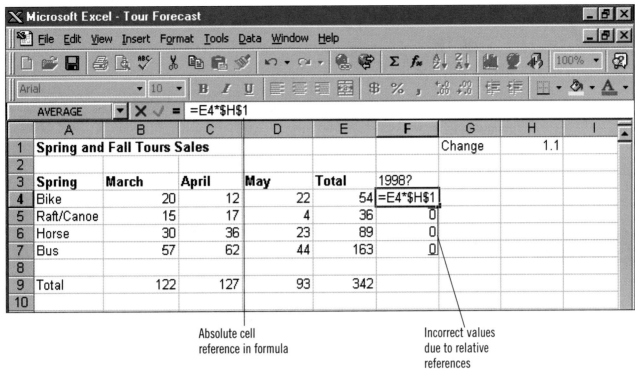

Absolute cell
reference in formula

Incorrect values
due to relative
references

FIGURE B-15: Worksheet with what-if value

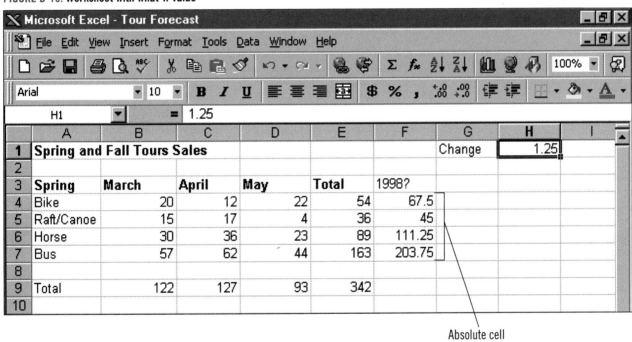

Absolute cell
reference in
formulas

CLUES TO USE

Project a What-If Analysis

The ability to "plug in" values in a worksheet means you can create countless what-if analyses. A what-if analysis occurs when you insert different values into a worksheet model. This type of analysis can help you determine budgetary constraints, and can influence corporate economic decisions.

Naming and Moving a Sheet

Each workbook initially contains three worksheets. When the workbook is opened, the first worksheet is the active sheet. To move from sheet to sheet, click the desired sheet tab located at the bottom of the worksheet window. Sheet tab scrolling buttons, located to the left of the sheet tabs, allow rapid movement among the sheets. To make it easier to identify the sheets in a workbook, you can name each sheet. The name appears on the sheet tab. For instance, sheets within a single workbook could be named for individual sales people to better track performance goals. To better organize a workbook, you can easily rearrange sheets within it. ◢◤ Evan wants to be able to easily identify the Tour Information and the Tour Forecast sheets. He decides to name the two sheets in his workbook, then changes their order.

Steps 1 2 3 4

1. Click the **Sheet1 tab**

Sheet1 becomes active; this is the worksheet that contains the Fall Tour Forecast information you compiled for the Marketing department. Its tab moves to the front, and the tab for Sheet2 moves to the background.

2. Click the **Sheet2 tab**

Sheet2, containing last year's Tour Information, becomes active. Now that you have confirmed which sheet is which, rename Sheet1 so it has a name that identifies its contents.

3. Double-click the **Sheet1 tab**

The Sheet1 text ("Sheet1") is selected. You could also click Format in the menu bar, point to Sheet, then click Rename to select the sheet name.

4. Type **Forecast**, then press **[Enter]**

See Figure B-16. The new name automatically replaced the default name on the tab. Worksheet names can have up to 31 characters, including spaces and punctuation.

5. Double-click the **Sheet2 tab**, then rename this sheet **Information**

You decide to rearrange the order of the sheets, so that Forecast comes after Information.

6. Drag the **Forecast sheet** after the **Information sheet**

As you drag, the pointer changes to a sheet relocation indicator.
See Figure B-17.

7. Save and close the workbook, then exit Excel

FIGURE B-16: **Renamed sheet in workbook**

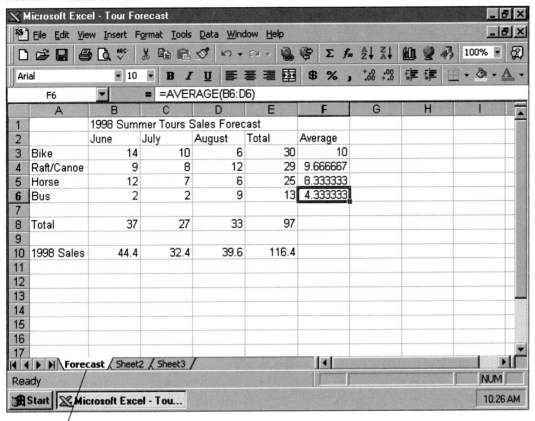

Sheet 1 renamed

FIGURE B-17: **Moving Forecast after Information sheet**

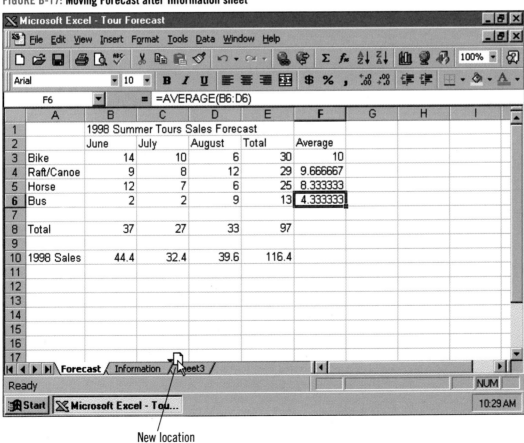

New location
indicator

Practice

► Concepts Review

Label each of the elements of the Excel worksheet window shown in Figure B-18.

FIGURE B-18

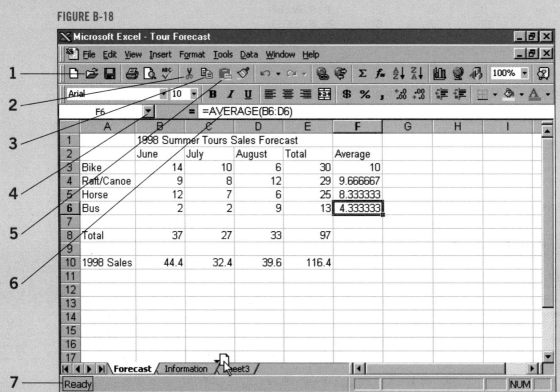

Match each of the terms with the statement that describes its function.

8. Range *C*

9. Function *a*

10. 📋 *e*

11. 📑 *d*

12. Formula *b*

a. A predefined formula that provides a shortcut for commonly used calculations

b. A cell entry that performs a calculation in an Excel worksheet

c. A specified group of cells, which can include the entire worksheet

d. Used to copy cells

e. Used to paste cells

Select the best answer from the list of choices.

13. **What type of cell reference changes when it is copied?**
    a. Absolute
    b. Circular
    c. Looping
    d. Relative

14. **Which character is used to make a reference absolute?**
    a. &
    b. ^
    c. $
    d. @

▶ Skills Review

1 Edit cell entries and work with ranges.
  a. Open workbook XL B-2 and save it as "Mutual Funds" on your Student Disk.
  b. Change the number of Arch shares to 210.
  c. Change the price per share of RST stock to 18.45.
  d. Change the number of United shares to 100.
  e. Name the range B2:B5 "Shares".
  f. Name the range C2:C5 "Price".
  g. Save, preview, and print your worksheet.

2 Enter formulas.
  a. Click cell B6.
  b. Enter the formula B2+B3+B4+B5.
  c. Click cell C6.
  d. Enter the formula C2+C3+C4+C5.
  e. Save your work, then preview and print the data in the Mutual Funds worksheet.

3 Introduce functions.
  a. Click cell C7.
  b. Enter the MIN function for the range C2:C5.
  c. Type the label Min Price in cell A7.
  d. Save your work.
  e. Preview and print this worksheet.

4 Copy and move cell entries.
  a. Select the range A1:E6.
  b. Use drag-and-drop to copy the range to cell A10.
  c. Delete the range B11:C14.
  d. Save your work.
  e. Preview and print this worksheet.

5 Copy formulas with relative cell references.

  a. Click cell D2.

  b. Create a formula that multiplies B2 and C2.

  c. Copy the formula in D2 into cells D3:D5.

  d. Copy the formula in D2 into cells D11:D14.

  e. Save, preview, and print this worksheet.

6 Copy formulas with absolute cell references.

  a. Click cell G2.

  b. Type the value 1.375.

  c. Click cell E2.

  d. Create a formula containing an absolute reference that multiplies D2 and G2.

  e. Copy the formula in E2 into cells E3:E5.

  f. Copy the formula in E2 into cells E11:E14.

  g. Change the amount in cell G2 to 2.873.

  h. Save, preview, and print this worksheet.

7 Name a sheet.

  a. Name the Sheet1 tab "Funds".

  b. Move the Funds sheet so it comes after Sheet3.

  c. Save and close this worksheet.

► Independent Challenges

1. You are the box-office manager for Lightwell Players, a regional theater company. Your responsibilities include tracking seasonal ticket sales for the company's main stage productions and anticipating ticket sales for the next season. Lightwell Players sells four types of tickets: reserved seating, general admission, senior citizen tickets, and student tickets. The 1993–94 season included productions of *Hamlet*, *The Cherry Orchard*, *Fires in the Mirror*, *The Shadow Box*, and *Heartbreak House*.

Open a new workbook and save it as "Theater" on your Student Disk. Plan and build a worksheet that tracks the sales of each of the four ticket types for all five of the plays. Calculate the total ticket sales for each play, the total sales for each of the four ticket types, and the total sales for all tickets.

Enter your own sales data, but assume the following: the Lightwell Players sold 800 tickets during the season; reserved seating was the most popular ticket type for all of the shows except for *The Shadow Box*; no play sold more than 10 student tickets. Plan and build a second worksheet in the workbook that reflects a 5% increase in sales of all ticket types.

To complete this independent challenge:

1. Think about the results you want to see, the information you need to build into these worksheets, and what types of calculations must be performed.
2. Sketch sample worksheets on a piece of paper to indicate how the information should be laid out. What information should go in the columns? In the rows?
3. Build the worksheets by entering a title, row labels, column headings, and formulas. Use named ranges to make the worksheet easier to use, and rename the sheet tabs to easily identify the contents of each sheet. (Hint: If your columns are too narrow, position the cell pointer in the column you want to widen. To widen the column, click Format on the menu bar, click Column, click Width, choose a new column width, and then click OK.)
4. Use separate worksheets for existing ticket sales and projected sales showing the 5% increase.
5. Save your work, then preview and print the worksheets.
6. Submit your sketches and printed worksheets.

2. You have been promoted to computer lab manager at your school, and it is your responsibility to make sure there are enough computers for students during scheduled classes. Currently, you have four classrooms: three with IBM PCs and one with Macintoshes. Classes are scheduled Monday, Wednesday, and Friday in two-hour increments from 9 a.m. to 5 p.m. (the lab closes at 7 p.m.), and each room can currently accommodate 20 computers.

Open a new workbook and save it as "Lab Manager" on your Student Disk. Plan and build a worksheet that tracks the number of students who can currently use available computers per two-hour class. Create your enrollment data, but assume that current enrollment averages 85% of each room's daily capacity. Using an additional worksheet, show the impact of an enrollment increase of 25%.

To complete this independent challenge:

1. Think about how to construct these worksheets to create the desired output.
2. Sketch sample paper worksheets, to indicate how the information should be laid out.
3. Build the worksheets by entering a title, row labels, column headings, and formulas. Use named ranges to make the worksheet easier to use, and rename the sheets to identify their contents easily.
4. Use separate sheets for actual enrollment and projected changes.
5. Save your work, then preview and print the worksheets.
6. Submit your sketches and printed worksheets.

3. Nuts and Bolts is a small but growing hardware store that has hired you to organize its accounting records using Excel. The store hopes to track its inventory using Excel once its accounting records are under control. Before you were hired, one of the accounting staff started to enter expenses in a workbook, but the work was never completed. Open the workbook XL B-3 and save it as "Nuts and Bolts Finances" on your Student Disk. Include functions such as the Average, Maximum, and Minimum amounts of each of the expenses in the worksheet.

To complete this independent challenge:

1. Think about what information would be important for the accounting staff to know.
2. Use the existing worksheet to create a paper sketch of the types of functions and formulas you will use and of where they will be located. Indicate where you will have named ranges.
3. Create your sketch using the existing worksheet as a foundation. Your worksheet should use range names in its formulas and functions.
4. Rename Sheet1 "Expenses".
5. Save your work, and then preview and print the worksheet.
6. Submit your sketches and printed worksheets.

4. The immediacy of the World Wide Web allows you to find comparative data on any service or industry of interest to you. Your company is interested in investing in one of any of the most actively traded stocks in the three primary trading houses, and you have been asked to retrieve this information. To complete this independent challenge:

1. Open a new workbook and save it on your Student Disk as Stock Data.
2. Log on to the Internet and use your browser to go to the http://www.course.com. From there, click the link Student On Line Companions, then click the Microsoft Office 97 Professional Edition — Illustrated: A First Course page, then click on the Excel link for Unit B.
3. Use each of the following sites to compile your data: NASDAQ [www.nasdaq.com], the New York Stock Exchange [www.nyse.com], and the American Stock Exchange [www.amex.com].
4. Using one worksheet per exchange, locate data for the 10 most actively traded stocks.
5. Make sure all stocks are identified using their commonly known names.
6. Your company will invest a total of $100,000 and wants to make that investment in only one exchange. Still, they are asking you to research the types of stocks that could be purchased in each exchange.
7. Assume an even distribution of the original investment in the stocks, and total pertinent columns. Determine the total number of shares that will be purchased.
8. Save, print, and hand in a print of your work.

► Visual Workshop

Create a worksheet similar to Figure B-19 using the skills you learned in this unit. Save the workbook as "Annual Budget" on your Student Disk. Preview, and then print the worksheet.

FIGURE B-19

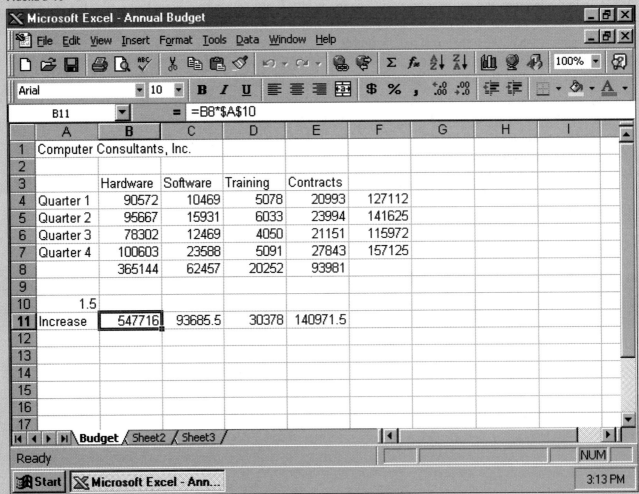

Formatting
a Worksheet

Objectives

► **Format values**
► **Select fonts and point sizes**
► **Change attributes and alignment of labels**
► **Adjust column widths**
► **Insert and delete rows and columns**
► **Apply colors, patterns, and borders**
► **Use conditional formatting**
► **Check spelling**

Now you will learn how to format a worksheet to make it easier to read and to emphasize key data. You do this by formatting cell contents, adjusting column widths, and inserting and deleting columns and rows. ✐▬ The marketing managers at Nomad Ltd have asked Evan Brillstein to create a worksheet that tracks tour advertising expenses. Evan has prepared a worksheet containing this information, and now he needs to use formatting techniques to make the worksheet easier to read and to call attention to important data.

Excel 97

Formatting Values

Formatting is how information appears in cells; it does not alter the data in any way. To format a cell, you select it, then apply the formatting you want. You can also format a range of cells. Cells and ranges can be formatted before or after data is entered. If you enter a value in a cell, and the cell appears to display the data incorrectly, you need to format the cell to display the value correctly. You might also want more than one cell to have the same format. ◀━━━ The Marketing Department has requested that Evan track tour advertising expenses. Evan developed a worksheet that tracks invoices for tour advertising. He has entered all the information and now wants to format some of the labels and values in the worksheet. Because some of the format changes he will make to labels and values might also affect column widths, Evan decided to make all his formatting changes before changing the column widths. He formats his values first.

Steps

1. **Open the worksheet XL C-1 from your Student Disk, then save it as Tour Ads**
   The tour advertising worksheet appears in Figure C-1.
   You want to format the data in the Cost ea. column so it displays with a dollar sign.

2. **Select the range E4:E32, then click the Currency Style button** 💲 **on the Formatting toolbar**
   Excel adds dollar signs and two decimal places to the Cost ea. column data. When the new format is applied, Excel automatically resizes the columns to display all the information. Columns G, H, and I contain dollar values also, but you decide to apply the comma format instead of currency.

3. **Select the range G4:I32, then click the Comma Style button** , **on the Formatting toolbar**
   Column J contains percentages.

4. **Select the range J4:J32, click the Percent Style button** % **on the Formatting toolbar, then click the Increase Decimal button** .00 **on the Formatting toolbar to show one decimal place**
   Data in the % of Total column is now formatted in Percent style. Next, you reformat the invoice dates.

5. **Select the range B4:B31, click Format on the menu bar, then click Cells**
   The Format Cells dialog box appears with the Number tab in front and the Date format already selected. See Figure C-2. You can also use this dialog box to format ranges with currency, commas, and percentages.

6. **Select the format 4-Mar-97 in the Type list box, then click OK**
   You decide you don't need the year to appear in the Inv Due column.

7. **Select the range C4:C31, click Format on the menu bar, click Cells, click 4-Mar in the Type list box, then click OK**
   Compare your worksheet to Figure C-3.

8. **Save your work**

FIGURE C-1: Tour advertising worksheet

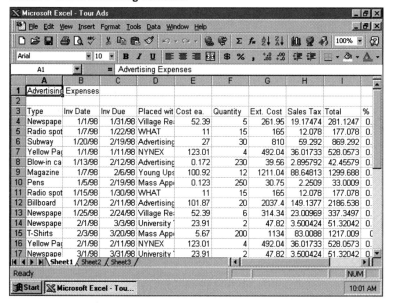

FIGURE C-2: Format Cells dialog box

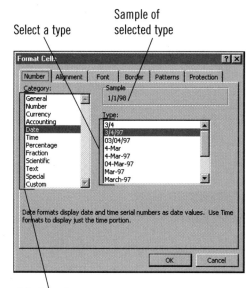

Select a type

Sample of selected type

Select a category

FIGURE C-3: Worksheet with formatted values

Currency Style button

Percent Style button

Comma Style button

Increase decimal button

Decrease decimal button

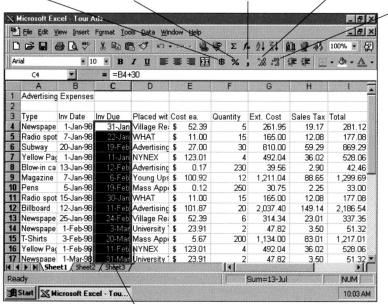

Modified date formats

Using the Format Painter

A cell's format can be "painted" into other cells using the Format Painter button on the Formatting toolbar. This is similar to using drag-and-drop to copy information, but instead of copying cell contents, you copy only the cell format. Select the cell containing the desired format, then click . The pointer changes to , as shown in Figure C-4. Use this pointer to select the cell or range you want to contain the painted format.

FIGURE C-4: Using the Format Painter

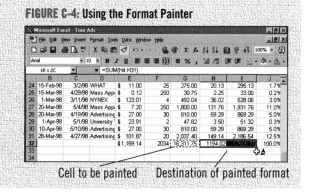

Cell to be painted   Destination of painted format

FORMATTING A WORKSHEET EX C-3 ◄

Selecting Fonts and Point Sizes

A **font** is the name given to a collection of characters (letters, numerals, symbols, and punctuation marks) with a specific design. The **point size** is the physical size of the text, measured in points. The default font in Excel is 10 point Arial. You can change the font, the size, or both of any entry or section in a worksheet by using the Format command on the menu bar or by using the Formatting toolbar. Table C-1 shows several fonts in different sizes. Now that the data is formatted, Evan wants to change the font and size of the labels and the worksheet title so that they stand out.

Steps

QuickTip

You can also open the Format Cells dialog box by right-clicking the mouse after selecting cells, then selecting Format Cells.

1. Press **[Ctrl][Home]** to select cell A1

2. Click **Format** on the menu bar, click **Cells**, then click the **Font tab** in the Format Cells dialog box
   See Figure C-5.
   You decide to change the font of the title from Arial to Times New Roman, and increase the font size to 24.

Trouble?

If you don't have Times New Roman in your list of fonts, choose another font.

3. Click **Times New Roman** in the Font list box, click **24** in the Size list box, then click **OK**
   The title font appears in 24 point Times New Roman, and the Formatting toolbar displays the new font and size information. Next, you make the column headings larger.

4. Select the range **A3:J3**, click **Format** on the menu bar, then click **Cells**
   The Font tab should still be the front-most tab in the Format Cells dialog box.

QuickTip

The Format Cells dialog box displays a sample of the selected font. Use the Format Cells command to access the Format Cells dialog box if you're unsure of a font's appearance.

5. Click **Times New Roman** in the Font list box, click **14** in the Size list box, then click **OK**
   Compare your worksheet to Figure C-6.

6. Save your work

TABLE C-1: Types of fonts

font	12 point	24 point
Arial	Excel	Excel
Helvetica	Excel	Excel
Palatino	Excel	Excel
Times	Excel	Excel

FIGURE C-5: Font tab in the Format Cells dialog box

Available fonts on your computer—yours may differ

Currently selected font

Font attribute options

Type a custom font size or select from the list

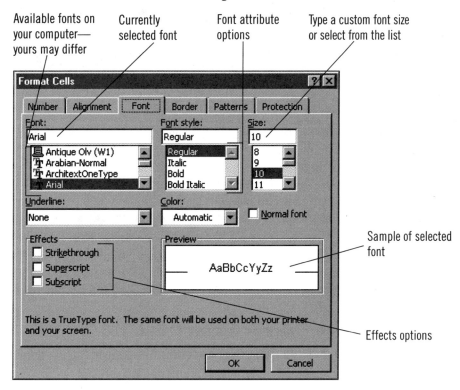

Sample of selected font

Effects options

FIGURE C-6: Worksheet with enlarged title and labels

Column headings now 14 point Times New Roman

Font and size of active cell

Title after changing to 24 point Times New Roman

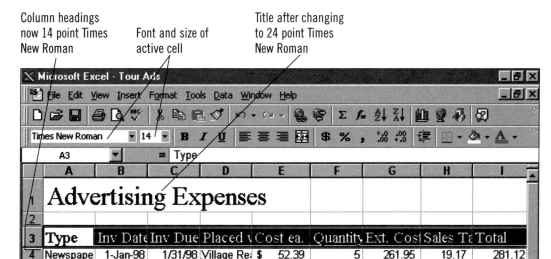

CLUES TO USE

Using the Formatting toolbar to change fonts and sizes

The font and size of the active cell appear on the Formatting toolbar. Click the Font list arrow, as shown in Figure C-7, to see a list of available fonts. If you want to change the font, first select the cell, click the Font list arrow, then choose the font you want. You can change the size of selected text in the same way, by clicking the Size list arrow on the Formatting toolbar to display a list of available point sizes.

FIGURE C-7: Available fonts on the Formatting toolbar

Available fonts installed on your computer—yours may differ

Excel 97

Changing Attributes and Alignment of Labels

Attributes are font styling features such as bold, italics, and underlining. You can apply bold, italics, and underlining from the Formatting toolbar or from the Font tab in the Format Cells dialog box. You can also change the alignment of text in cells. Left, right, or center alignment can be applied from the Formatting toolbar, or from the Alignment tab in the Format Cells dialog box. See Table C-2 for a description of the available attribute and alignment buttons on the Formatting toolbar. Excel also has predefined worksheet formats to make formatting easier. ◢◣ Now that he has applied the appropriate fonts and font sizes to his worksheet labels, Evan wants to further enhance his worksheet's appearance by adding bold and underline formatting and centering some of the labels.

1. Press **[Ctrl][Home]** to select cell A1, then click the **Bold button** [B] on the Formatting toolbar
The title "Advertising Expenses" appears in bold.

2. Select the range **A3:J3**, then click the **Underline button** [U] on the Formatting toolbar
Excel underlines the column headings in the selected range.

QuickTip

Highlighting information on a worksheet can be useful, but overuse of any attribute can be distracting and make a document less readable. Be consistent by adding emphasis the same way throughout a workbook.

3. Click cell **A3**, click the **Italics button** [I] on the Formatting toolbar, then click [B]
The word "Type" appears in boldface, italic type. Notice that the Bold, Italics, and Underline buttons on the Formatting toolbar are indented. You decide you don't like the italic formatting. You remove it by clicking [I] again.

4. Click [I]
Excel removes italics from cell A3.

5. Add bold formatting to the rest of the labels in the range **B3:J3**
You want to center the title over the data.

6. Select the range **A1:F1**, then click the **Merge and Center button** [▦] on the Formatting toolbar
The title Advertising Expenses is centered across six columns. Now you center the column headings in their cells.

Time To

✔ Save

7. Select the range **A3:J3** then click the **Center button** [≡] on the Formatting toolbar
You are satisfied with the formatting in the worksheet.
Compare your screen to Figure C-8.

FIGURE C-8: Worksheet with formatting attributes applied

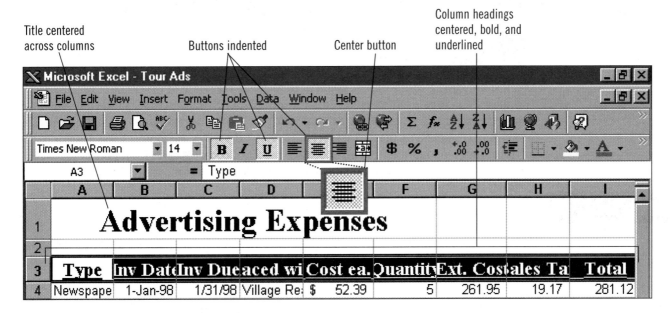

Title centered across columns

Buttons indented

Center button

Column headings centered, bold, and underlined

TABLE C-2: Attribute and Alignment buttons on the Formatting toolbar

icon	description	icon	description
B	Adds boldface		Aligns left
I	Italicizes		Aligns center
U	Underlines		Aligns right
	Adds lines or borders		Centers across columns, and combines two or more selected adjacent cells into one cell.

Using AutoFormat

Excel provides 16 preset formats called AutoFormats, which allow instant formatting of large amounts of data. AutoFormats are designed for worksheets with labels in the left column and top rows and totals in the bottom row or right column. To use AutoFormatting, select the data to be formatted—or place your mouse pointer anywhere within the range to be selected—click Format on the menu bar, click AutoFormat, then select a format from the Table Format list box, as shown in Figure C-9.

FIGURE C-9: AutoFormat dialog box

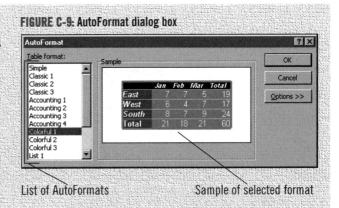

List of AutoFormats

Sample of selected format

Excel 97

Adjusting Column Widths

As you work with a worksheet, you might need to adjust the width of the columns to make your worksheet more usable. The default column width is 8.43 characters wide, a little less than one inch. With Excel, you can adjust the column width for one or more columns using the mouse or the Column command on the Format menu. Table C-3 describes the commands available on the Format Column menu. You can also adjust the height of rows. Evan notices that some of the labels in column A don't fit in the cells. He decides to adjust the widths of columns so that the labels fit in the cells.

Steps

1. **Position the pointer on the column line between columns A and B in the column header area**
   The pointer changes to ↔, as shown in Figure C-10. You make the column wider.

2. **Drag the line to the right until column A is wide enough to accommodate all of the labels for types of advertising**
   You decide to resize the columns so they automatically accommodate the widest entry in a cell.

3. **Position the pointer on the column line between columns B and C in the column header area until it changes to ↔, then double-click the left mouse button**
   The width of column B is automatically resized to fit the widest entry, in this case, the column head. This feature is called **AutoFit**.

4. **Repeat step 3 to use AutoFit to automatically resize columns C, D, and J**
   You can also use the Column Width command on the Format menu to adjust several columns to the same width.

5. **Select the range F5:I5**
   Any cells in the columns you want to resize can be selected.

6. **Click Format on the menu bar, point to Column, then click Width**
   The Column Width dialog box appears. Move the dialog box, if necessary, by dragging it by its title bar so you can see the contents of the worksheet.

7. **Type 12 in the Column Width text box, then click OK**
   The column widths change to reflect the new settings. See Figure C-11. You are satisfied and decide to save the worksheet.

8. **Save your work**

> **QuickTip**
>
> To reset columns to the default width, select the range of cells, then use the Column Standard Width command on the Format menu. Click OK in the Standard Width dialog box to accept the default width.

TABLE C-3: Format Column commands

command	description
Width	Sets the width to a specific number of characters
AutoFit Selection	Fits the widest entry
Hide	Hide(s) column(s)
Unhide	Unhide(s) column(s)
Standard Width	Resets to default widths

FIGURE C-10: Preparing to change the column width

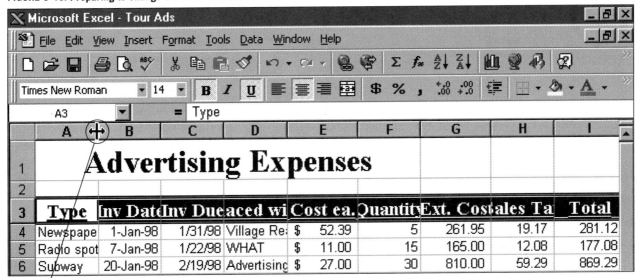

Resize pointer
between columns
A and B

FIGURE C-11: Worksheet with column widths adjusted

Placed with	Cost ea.	Quantity	Ext. Cost	Sales Tax	Total	% of
Village Reader	$ 52.39	5	261.95	19.17	281.12	
WHAT	$ 11.00	15	165.00	12.08	177.08	
Advertising Concepts	$ 27.00	30	810.00	59.29	869.29	
NYNEX	$ 123.01	4	492.04	36.02	528.06	
Advertising Concepts	$ 0.17	230	39.56	2.90	42.46	

Specifying row height

The Row Height command on the Format menu allows you to customize row height to improve readability. Row height is calculated in points, units of measure also used for fonts—one inch equals 72 points. The row height must exceed the size of the font you are using. For example, if you are using a 12 point font, the row height must be more than 12 points. Normally, you don't need to adjust row heights manually. If you format something in a row to be a larger point size, Excel will adjust the row height to fit the largest point size in the row.

Inserting and Deleting Rows and Columns

As you modify a worksheet, you might find it necessary to insert or delete rows and columns. For example, you might need to insert rows to accommodate new inventory products or remove a column of yearly totals that are no longer current. Inserting or deleting rows or columns can help to make your worksheet more readable. Evan has already improved the appearance of his worksheet by formatting the labels and values in the worksheet. Now he decides to improve the overall appearance of the worksheet by inserting a row between the last row of data and the totals. This will help make the totals stand out more. Evan has also located a row of inaccurate data that should be deleted.

QuickTip

Inserting or deleting rows or columns can also cause problems with formulas that reference cells in that area, so be sure to consider this when inserting or deleting rows or columns.

1. Click cell **A32**, click **Insert** on the menu bar, then click **Cells**

The Insert dialog box opens. See Figure C-12. You can choose to insert a column or a row, or you can shift the data in the cells in the active column right or in the active row down. You want to insert a row to add some space between the last row of data and the totals.

2. Click the **Entire Row radio button**, then click **OK**

A blank row is inserted between the title and the month labels. When you insert a new row, the contents of the worksheet shift down from the newly inserted row. When you insert a new column, the contents of the worksheet shift to the right from the point of the new column. Now delete the row containing information about hats, as this information is inaccurate.

3. Click the **row 27 selector button** (the gray box containing the row number to the left of the worksheet)

All of row 27 is selected as shown in Figure C-13.

4. Click **Edit** on the menu bar, then click **Delete**

Excel deletes row 27, and all rows below this shift up one row. You are satisfied with the appearance of the worksheet.

5. Save your work

FIGURE C-12: Insert dialog box

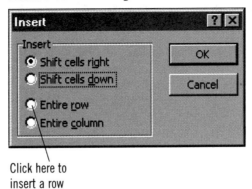

```
Insert                           ? X
 ─Insert────────────
  ● Shift cells right        ┌──────────┐
  ○ Shift cells down         │    OK    │
                             └──────────┘
  ○ Entire row               ┌──────────┐
  ○ Entire column            │  Cancel  │
                             └──────────┘
```

Click here to
insert a row

FIGURE C-13: Worksheet with row 27 selected

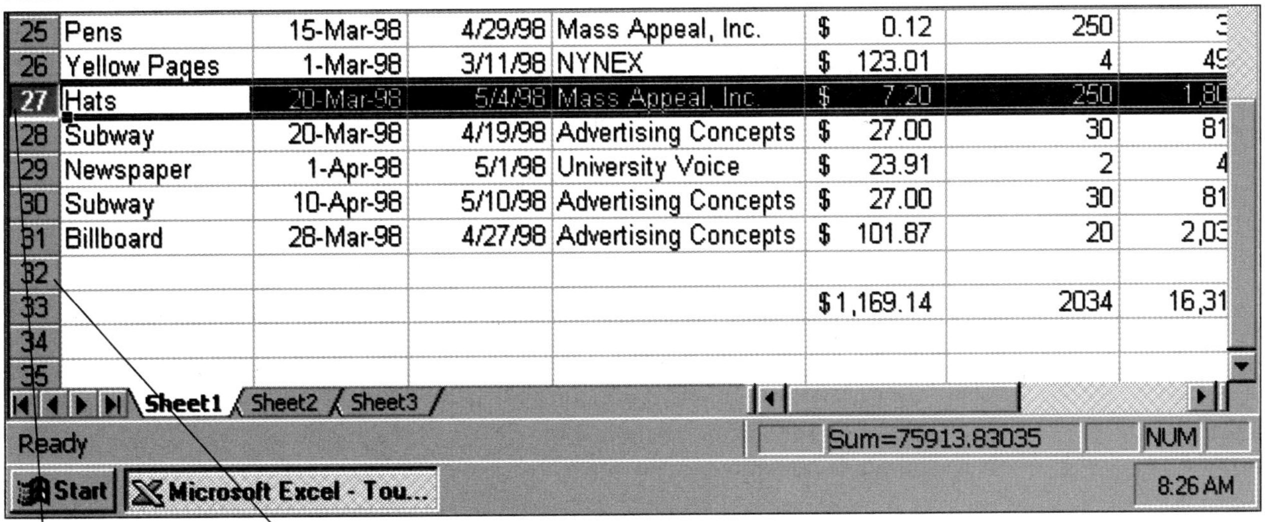

25	Pens	15-Mar-98	4/29/98	Mass Appeal, Inc.	$ 0.12	250	3
26	Yellow Pages	1-Mar-98	3/11/98	NYNEX	$ 123.01	4	49
27	Hats	20-Mar-98	5/4/98	Mass Appeal, Inc.	$ 7.20	250	1,80
28	Subway	20-Mar-98	4/19/98	Advertising Concepts	$ 27.00	30	81
29	Newspaper	1-Apr-98	5/1/98	University Voice	$ 23.91	2	4
30	Subway	10-Apr-98	5/10/98	Advertising Concepts	$ 27.00	30	81
31	Billboard	28-Mar-98	4/27/98	Advertising Concepts	$ 101.87	20	2,03
32							
33					$1,169.14	2034	16,31
34							
35							

Sheet1 / Sheet2 / Sheet3

Ready   Sum=75913.83035   NUM

Start   Microsoft Excel - Tou...   8:26 AM

Row 27 selector   Inserted row
button

Excel 97

Using dummy columns and rows

You use cell references and ranges in formulas. When you add or delete a column or row within a range used in a formula, Excel automatically adjusts the formula to reflect the change. However, when you add a column or row at the end of a range used in a formula, you must modify the formula to reflect the additional column or row. To avoid having to edit the formula, you can include a dummy column and dummy row within the range you use for that formula. A dummy column is a blank column included to the right of but within a range. A dummy row is a blank row included at the bottom of but within a range, as shown in Figure C-14. Then if you add another column or row to the end of the range, the formula will automatically be modified to include the new data.

FIGURE C-14: Formula with dummy row

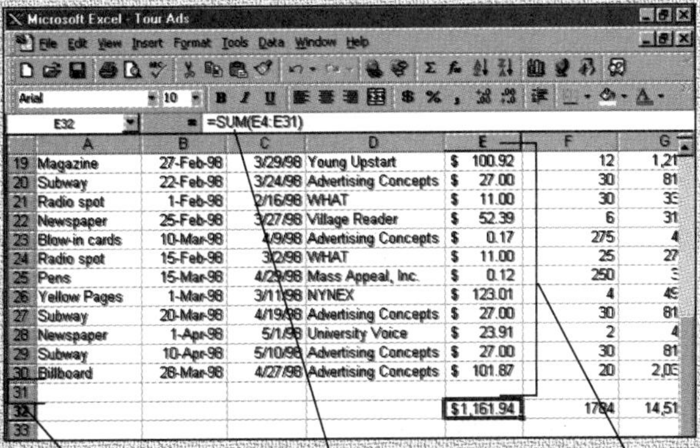

Dummy row   Formula with   Rows included
             dummy row   in formula

FORMATTING A WORKSHEET EX C-11

Applying Colors, Patterns, and Borders

You can use colors, patterns, and borders to enhance the overall appearance of a worksheet and to improve its readability. You can add these enhancements using the Patterns tab in the Format Cells dialog box or by using the Borders and Color buttons on the Formatting toolbar. When you use the Format Cells dialog box, you can see what your enhanced text will look like in the Sample box. You can apply color to the background of a cell or range or to cell contents. If you do not have a color monitor, the colors appear in shades of gray. You can apply patterns to the background of a cell or range. And, you can apply borders to all the cells in a worksheet or only to selected cells. See Table C-4 for a list of border buttons and their functions. ✐ Evan decides to add a pattern, a border, and color to the title of the worksheet. This will give the worksheet a more professional appearance.

1. Click cell **A1**, then click the **Fill Color button list arrow** 🖌️ ▾ on the Formatting toolbar
The color palette appears, as shown in Figure C-15.

QuickTip

Use color sparingly. Excessive use can divert the reader's attention away from the data in the worksheet.

2. Click **Turquoise** (fourth row, fourth color from the right)

3. Click **Format** on the menu bar, then click **Cells**
The Format Cells dialog box opens.

4. Click the **Patterns tab**, as shown in Figure C-16, if it is not already displayed
When choosing a background pattern, consider that the more cell contents contrast with the background, the more readable the contents will be: You choose the diamond pattern.

5. Click the **Pattern list arrow**, click the **thin diagonal crosshatch pattern** (third row, last pattern on the right), then click **OK**
Now you add a border.

6. Click the **Borders button list arrow** ▦ ▾ on the Formatting toolbar, then click the **heavy bottom border** (second row, second border from the left)
Next, you change the font color.

7. Click the **Font Color button list arrow** 🅰 ▾ on the Formatting toolbar, then click **blue** (second row, third color from the right)
The text changes color, as shown in Figure C-17.

Time To

✔ Save

8. Preview and print the first page of the worksheet

TABLE C-4: Border buttons

button	description	button	description
▦	No border	▢	Thin border around range
▦	Single underline	▦	Left border
▦	Double underline	▦	Right border
▦	Thick bottom, thin top border	▦	Double bottom, single top
⊞	Outline all in range	▦	Thick bottom border
▣	Thick border around range		

FIGURE C-15: Fill Color palette

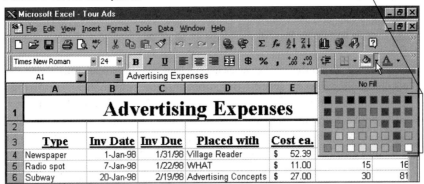

Choose from available colors

FIGURE C-16: Patterns tab in the Format Cells dialog box

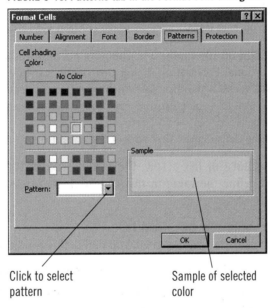

Click to select pattern

Sample of selected color

FIGURE C-17: Worksheet with color, patterns, and border

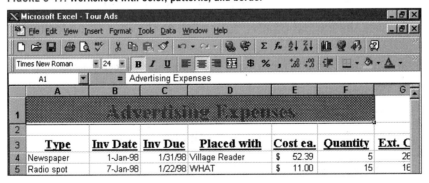

Using color to organize a worksheet

You can use color to give a distinctive look to each part of a worksheet. For example, you might want to apply a light blue to all the rows containing the subway data and a light green to all the rows containing the newspaper data. Be consistent throughout a group of worksheets, and try to avoid colors that are too bright and distracting.

Using Conditional Formatting

Formatting attributes make worksheets look professional, and these same attributes can be applied depending on specific outcomes in cells. Automatically applying formatting attributes based on cell values is called **conditional formatting.** You might, for example, want advertising costs above a certain number to display in red boldface, and lower values to display in blue. Evan wants his worksheet to include conditional formatting so that extended advertising costs greater than $175 display in red boldface. He creates the conditional format in the first cell in the extended cost column.

Steps

Trouble?

If the Office Assistant appears, click the No, don't provide help now button to close the Office Assistant.

1. Click cell **G4**
Use the scroll bars if necessary, to make column G visible.

2. Click **Format** on the menu bar, then click **Conditional Formatting**
The Conditional Formatting dialog box opens, as shown in Figure C-18. The number of input fields varies depending on which operator is selected. You can define up to 3 different conditions that let you determine outcome parameters and then assign formatting attributes to each one.
You begin by defining the first part of the condition.

3. Click the **Operator list arrow, then click greater than or equal to**
Next, you define the value in this condition that must be met for the formatting to be applied.

4. Click the **Value text box, then type 175**
Once the value has been assigned, you define this condition's formatting attributes.

5. Click **Format,** click the **Color list arrow,** click **Red** (third row, first color from the left), click **Bold** in the Font Style list box, click **OK,** then click **OK** again to close the Conditional Formatting dialog box
Next, you copy the formatting to the other cells in the column.

6. Click the **Format Painter button** ![icon] on the Formatting toolbar, then select the range **G5:G30**
Once the formatting is copied, you reposition the cell pointer to review the results.

7. Click cell **G4**
Compare your results to Figure C-19.

8. Press **[Ctrl][Home]** to move to cell AI

9. Save your work

FIGURE C-18: **Conditional Formatting dialog box**

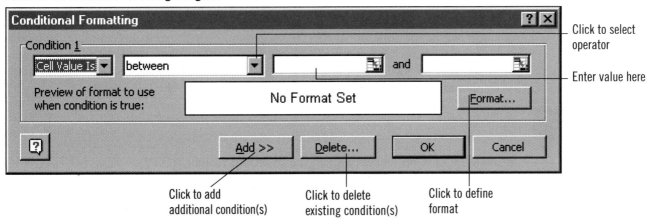

Click to select operator

Enter value here

Click to add additional condition(s)

Click to delete existing condition(s)

Click to define format

FIGURE C-19: **Worksheet with conditional formatting**

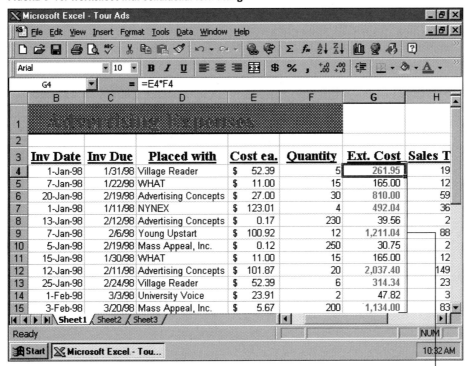

Results of conditional formatting

Deleting conditional formatting

Because its likely that the conditions you define will change, any of the conditional formats defined can be deleted. Select the cell(s) containing conditional formatting, click Format, click Conditional Formatting, then click the Delete button. The Delete Conditional Format dialog box opens, as shown in Figure C-20. Click the checkboxes for any of the conditions you want to delete, then click OK. The previously assigned formatting is deleted—leaving the cell's contents intact.

FIGURE C-20: **Delete Conditional Format dialog box**

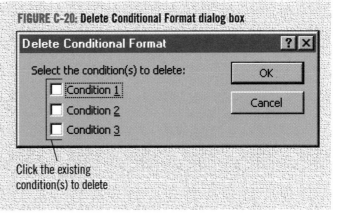

Click the existing condition(s) to delete

Excel 97

Checking Spelling

You may think your worksheet is complete, but if you haven't checked for spelling errors, you risk undermining the professional effect of your work. A single misspelled word can ruin your work. The spell checker in Excel is also shared by Word, PowerPoint, and Access, so any words you've added to the dictionary using those programs are also available in Excel. ◀━━ Evan has completed the formatting for his worksheet and is ready to check its spelling.

Steps

1. **Click the Spelling button ⬚ on the Standard toolbar**
   The Spelling dialog opens, as shown in Figure C-21, with the abbreviation Inv selected as the first misspelled word in the worksheet. The spell checker starts from the active cell and compares words in the worksheet to those in its dictionary. Any word not found in the dictionary causes the spell checker to stop. At that point, you can decide to Ignore, Change, or Add the word.
   You decide to Ignore All cases of Inv, the abbreviation of invoice.

2. **Click Ignore All, then click Ignore All again when the spell checker stops on T-Shirts**
   The spell checker found the word 'cards' misspelled. You find the correct spelling and fix the error.

3. **Scroll through the Suggestions list, click Cards, then click Change**
   The word 'Concepts' is also misspelled. Make this correction.

4. **Click Concepts in the Suggestions list, then click Change**
   When no more incorrect words are found, Excel displays the message box shown in Figure C-22.

5. **Click OK**

6. **Press [Ctrl][Home] to move to cell A1**

7. **Save your work**

8. **Preview and print the worksheet, then close the workbook and exit Excel**

FIGURE C-21: Spelling dialog box

Misspelled word

Type replacement word here or click a suggestion

Click to add word to dictionary

Click to ignore all occurrences of misspelled word

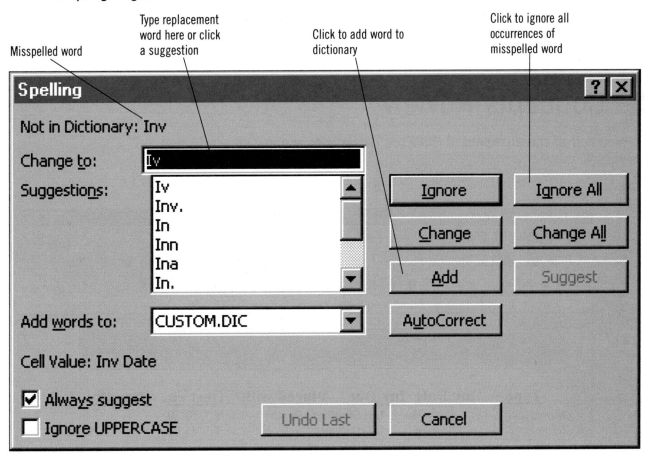

FIGURE C-22: Spelling completed warning box

Modifying the spell checker

Each of us use words specific to our profession or task. Because the dictionary supplied with Microsoft Office cannot possibly include all the words that each of us needs, it is possible to add words to the dictionary shared by all the components in the suite.

To customize the Microsoft Office dictionary used by the spell checker, click Add when a word not in the dictionary is found. From then on, that word will no longer be considered misspelled by the spell checker.

Practice

► Concepts Review

Label each of the elements of the Excel worksheet window shown in Figure C-23.

FIGURE C-23

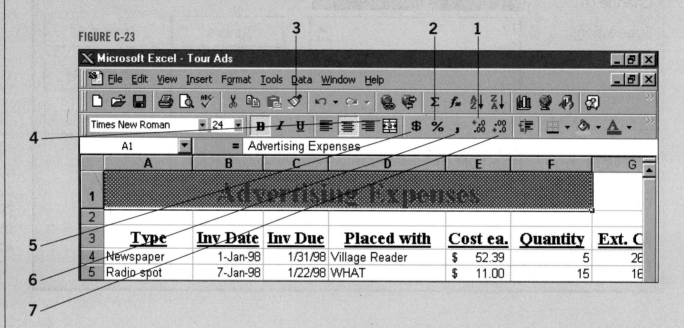

Match each of the statements to the command or button it describes.

8. Format Cells *d*	a. Adds a new row or column
9. Edit Clear *b*	b. Erases the contents of a cell
10. Insert Row/Column *a*	c. Checks the spelling in a worksheet
11. 📋 *e*	d. Changes the point size of selected cells
12. $ *f*	e. Pastes the contents of the Clipboard in the current cell
13. 📝 *c*	f. Changes the format to Currency

Select the best answer from the list of choices.

14. Which button increases the number of decimal places in selected cells?

a. [icon] b. [icon] c. [icon] d. [icon]

15. Each of the following operators can be used in conditional formatting, *except*

a. equal to   b. greater than   c. similar to   d. not between

16. How many conditional formats can be created in any cell?

a. 1   b. 2   c. 3   d. 4

▶ Skills Review

1. Format values.
   a. Open a new workbook.
   b. Enter the information from Table C-5 in your worksheet. Make sure you put "Quarterly Sales Sheet" on the next line.
   c. Select the range of values in the Price and Totals columns.
   d. Click the Currency Style button.
   e. Calculate the Totals column by multiplying the price by the number sold.
   f. Save this workbook as Chairs on your Student Disk.

TABLE C-5

Country Oak Chairs, Inc. Quarterly Sales Sheet			
Description	**Price**	**Sold**	**Totals**
Rocker	1299	1104	
Recliner	800	1805	
Bar stool	159	1098	
Dinette	369	1254	

2. Select fonts and point sizes.
   a. Select the range of cells containing the column titles.
   b. Change the font of the column titles to Times New Roman.
   c. Increase the point size of the column titles to 14 point.
   d. Resize columns as necessary.
   e. Save your workbook changes.

3. Change attributes and alignment of labels.
   a. Select the worksheet title Country Oak Chairs, Inc.
   b. Click the Bold button to apply boldface to the title.
   c. Select the label Quarterly Sales Sheet.
   d. Click the Underline button to apply underlining to the label.
   e. Add the bold attribute to the furniture descriptions, as well as the Totals label.
   f. Make the Price and Sold labels italics.
   g. Select the range of cells containing the column titles.
   h. Click the Center button to center the column titles.
   i. Save your changes, then preview and print the worksheet.

4. Adjust column widths.
   a. Change the width of the Price column to 11.
   b. Use the Format menu to make the Description and Sold columns the same size as the Price column.
   c. Save your workbook changes.

5. Insert and delete rows and columns.

a. Insert a new row between rows 4 and 5.

b. Add Country Oak Chairs' newest product—a Shaker bench—in the newly inserted row. Enter "239" for the price and "360" for the number sold.

c. Use the fill handle to copy the formula in cell D4 to D5.

d. Save your changes, then preview and print the workbook.

6. Apply colors, patterns, and borders.

a. Add a border around the data entered from Table C-5.

b. Apply a light green background color to the Descriptions column.

c. Apply a light pattern to the Descriptions column.

d. Apply a dark green background to the column labels.

e. Change the color of the font in the first row of the data to light green.

f. Save your work.

g. Preview and print the worksheet, then close the workbook.

7. Use conditional formatting.

a. Open the file XL C-2 from your Student Disk.

b. Save it as "Recap" on your Student Disk.

c. Create conditional formatting that changes values to blue if they are greater than 35000, and changes values to green if they are less than 21000.

d. Use the Bold button and Center button to format the column headings and row titles.

e. Autofit the other columns as necessary.

f. Save your changes.

8. Check spelling.

a. Open the spell checker.

b. Check the spelling in the worksheet.

c. Correct any spelling errors.

d. Save your changes, then preview and print the workbook.

e. Close the workbook, then exit Excel.

▶ Independent Challenges

1. Nuts and Bolts is a small but growing hardware store that has hired you to organize its accounting records using Excel. Now that the Nuts and Bolts hardware store's accounting records are on Excel, they would like you to work on the inventory. Although more items will be added later, enough have been entered in a worksheet for you to begin your modifications.

Open the workbook XL C-3 on your Student Disk, and save it as "NB Inventory."

To complete this independent challenge:

1. Create a formula that calculates the Value of the inventory on-hand for each item.
2. Use an absolute reference to calculate the Sale Price of each item.
3. Use enhancements to make the title, column headings, and row headings more attractive.
4. Make sure all columns are wide enough to see the data.
5. Before printing, preview the file so you know what the worksheet will look like. Adjust any items as needed, check spelling, and print a copy. Save your work before closing the file.
6. Submit your final printout.

2. You recently moved to a small town and joined the Chamber of Commerce. Since the other members are not computer-literate, you volunteered to organize the member organizations in a worksheet. As part of your efforts with the Chamber of Commerce, you need to examine more closely the membership in comparison to the community. To make the existing data more professional-looking and easier to read, you've decided to use attributes and your formatting abilities.

Open the workbook XL C-4 on your Student Disk, and save it as "Community."

To complete this independent challenge:

1. Remove any blank columns.
2. Format the Annual Revenue column using the Currency format.
3. Make all columns wide enough to fit their data.
4. Use formatting enhancements, such as fonts, font sizes, and text attributes, to make the worksheet more attractive.
5. Before printing, preview the file so you know what the worksheet will look like. Adjust any items as needed, check spelling, and print a copy. Save your work before closing the file.
6. Submit your final printout.

3. Write Brothers is a Houston-based company that manufactures high-quality pens and markers. As the finance manager, one of your responsibilities is to analyze the monthly reports from your five district sales offices. Your boss, Joanne Parker, has just told you to prepare a quarterly sales report for an upcoming meeting. Because several top executives will be attending this meeting, Joanne reminds you that the report must look professional. In particular, she asks you to emphasize the company's surge in profits during the last month and to highlight the fact that the Northeastern district continues to outpace the other districts.

Plan and build a worksheet that shows the company's sales during the last three months. Make sure you include:

- The number of pens sold (units sold) and the associated revenues (total sales) for each of the five district sales offices. The five Write Brothers sales districts include: Northeastern, Midwestern, Southeastern, Southern, and Western.
- Calculations that show month-by-month totals and a three-month cumulative total.
- Calculations that show each district's share of sales (percent of units sold).
- Formatting enhancements to emphasize the recent month's sales surge and the Northeastern district's sales leadership.

To complete this independent challenge:

1. Prepare a worksheet plan that states your goal, lists the worksheet data you'll need, and identifies the formulas for the different calculations.
2. Sketch a sample worksheet on a piece of paper, indicating how the information should be organized and formatted. How will you calculate the totals? What formulas can you copy to save time and keystrokes? Do any of these formulas need to use an absolute reference? How will you show dollar amounts? What information should be shown in bold? Do you need to use more than one font? More than one point size?
3. Build the worksheet with your own sales data. Enter the titles and labels first, then enter the numbers and formulas. Save the workbook as Write Brothers on your Student Disk.
4. Make enhancements to the worksheet. Adjust the column widths as necessary. Format labels and values, and change attributes and alignment.
5. Add a column that calculates a 10% increase in sales. Use an absolute cell reference in this calculation.
6. Before printing, preview the file so you know what the worksheet will look like. Adjust any items as needed, check spelling, and print a copy. Save your work before closing the file.
7. Submit your worksheet plan, preliminary sketches, and the final printout.

4. As the manager of your company's computer lab, you've been asked to assemble data on currently available software for use in a business environment. Using the World Wide Web, you can retrieve information about current software and create an attractive worksheet for distribution to department managers. To complete this independent challenge:

1. Open a new workbook and save it on your Student Disk as Software Comparison.
2. Log on to the Internet and use your browser to go to http://www.course.com. From there, click the link Student On Line Companions, then click the Microsoft Office 97 Professional Edition—Illustrated: A First Course page, then click the Excel link for Unit C.
3. Use each of the following sites to compile your data.
   Microsoft Corporation [www.microsoft.com], and Lotus Corporation [www.lotus.com].
4. Retrieve information on word processors, spreadsheets, presentation graphics, and database programs manufactured by both companies. The software must be Windows 95 compatible.
5. Create a worksheet that includes the information in step 4 above, as well as a retail price for each component, and whether all the programs can be purchased as a suite.
6. Use formatting attributes to make this data look attractive.
7. Use conditional formatting so that individual programs that cost over $100 display in red.
8. Save, print, and hand in a print out of your work.

▶ Visual Workshop

Create the following worksheet using the skills you learned in this unit. Open the file XL C-5 on your Student Disk, and save it as January Invoices. Create a conditional format in the Cost ea. column where entries greater than 50 are displayed in red. (Hint: The only additional font used in this exercise is Times New Roman. It is 22 points in row 1, and 14 points in row 3.)

FIGURE C-24

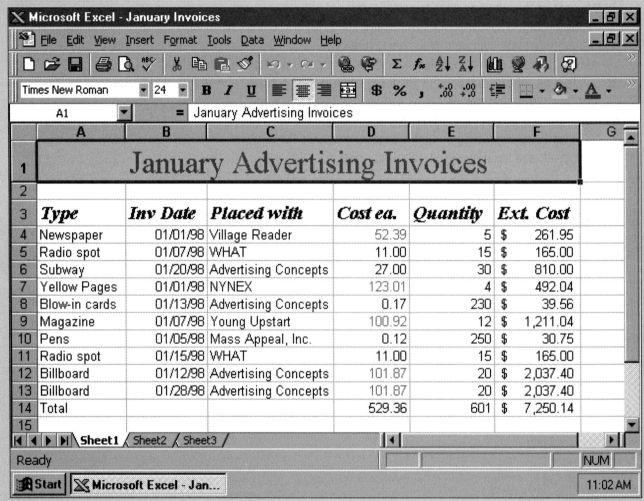

Working
with Charts

Objectives

- ► **Plan and design a chart**
- ► **Create a chart**
- ► **Move and resize a chart and its objects**
- ► **Edit a chart**
- ► **Change the appearance of a chart**
- ► **Enhance a chart**
- ► **Add text annotations and arrows to a chart**
- ► **Preview and print a chart**

Worksheets provide an effective way to organize information, but they are not always the best format for presenting data to others. Information in a selected range or worksheet can be easily converted to the visual format of a chart. Charts quickly communicate the relationships of data in a worksheet. In this unit, you will learn how to create a chart, edit a chart and change the chart type, add text annotations and arrows to a chart, then preview and print it. ◢ Evan Brillstein needs to create a chart showing the six-month sales history of Nomad Ltd for the annual meeting. He wants to illustrate the impact of an advertising campaign that started in June.

Planning and Designing a Chart

Before creating a chart, you need to plan what you want your chart to show and how you want it to look. ✏️ Evan wants to create a chart to be used at the annual meeting. The chart will show the spring and summer sales throughout the Nomad Ltd regions. In early June, the Marketing Department launched a national advertising campaign. The results of the campaign were increased sales for the summer months. Evan wants his chart to illustrate this dramatic sales increase. Evan uses the worksheet shown in Figure D-1 and the following guidelines to plan the chart:

Steps

CourseHelp

The camera icon indicates there is a CourseHelp for this lesson. Click the Start button, point to Programs, then click Excel 97 Illustrated. Choose the CourseHelp that corresponds to this lesson.

1. **Determine the purpose of the chart, and identify the data relationships you want to communicate visually**
   You want to create a chart that shows sales throughout Nomad's regions in the spring and summer months (March through August). In particular, you want to highlight the increase in sales that occurred in the summer months as a result of the advertising campaign.

2. **Determine the results you want to see, and decide which chart type is most appropriate to use; Table D-1 describes several different types of charts**
   Because you want to compare related data (sales in each of the regions) over a time period (the months March through August), you decide to use a column chart.

3. **Identify the worksheet data you want the chart to illustrate**
   You are using data from the worksheet titled "Nomad Ltd Regions, Spring and Summer Sales," as shown in Figure D-1. This worksheet contains the sales data for the five regions from March through August.

4. **Sketch the chart, then use your sketch to decide where the chart elements should be placed**
   You sketch your chart as shown in Figure D-2. You put the months on the horizontal axis (the **X-axis**) and the monthly sales figures on the vertical axis (the **Y-axis**). The **tick marks** on the Y-axis create a scale of measure for each value. Each value in a cell you select for your chart is a **data point**. In any chart, each data point is visually represented by a **data marker**, which in this case is a column. A collection of related data points is a **data series**. In this chart, there are five data series (Midwest, Northeast, Northwest, South, and Southwest), so you have included a **legend** to identify them.

FIGURE D-1: **Worksheet containing sales data**

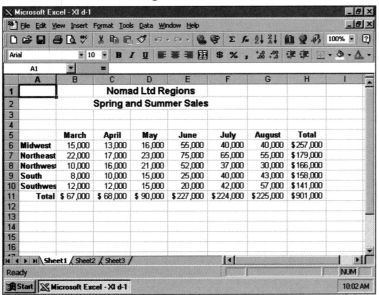

FIGURE D-2: **Sketch of the column chart**

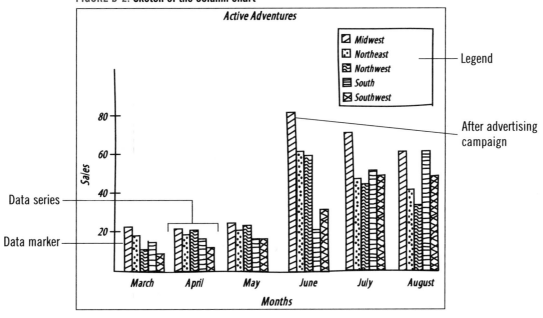

TABLE D-1: **Commonly used chart types**

type	button	description
Area		Shows how volume changes over time
Bar		Compares distinct, unrelated objects over time using a horizontal format; sometimes referred to as a horizontal bar chart in other spreadsheet programs
Column		Compares distinct, unrelated objects over time using a vertical format; the Excel default; sometimes referred to as a bar chart in other spreadsheet programs
Line		Compares trends over even time intervals; similar to an area chart
Pie		Compares sizes of pieces as part of a whole; can have slices pulled away from the pie, or "exploded"
XY (scatter)		Compares trends over uneven time or measurement intervals; used in scientific and engineering disciplines for trend spotting and extrapolation
Combination	none	Combines a column and line chart to compare data requiring different scales of measure

Creating a Chart

To create a chart in Excel, you first select the range containing the data you want to chart. Once you've selected a range, you can use Excel's Chart Wizard to lead you through the chart creation process. ◆◆◆ Using the worksheet containing the spring and summer sales data for the five regions, Evan will create a chart that shows the monthly sales of each region from March through August.

1. **Open the workbook XL D-1 from your Student Disk, then save it as Nomad Regions**
   First, you need to select the cells you want to chart. You want to include the monthly sales figures for each of the regions, but not the totals. You also want to include the month and region labels.

QuickTip

When selecting a large, unnamed range, select the upper left-most cell in the range, press and hold [Shift], then click the lower right-most cell in the range.

2. **Select the range A5:G10, then click the Chart Wizard button 📊 on the Standard toolbar**
   When you click 📊 the Chart Wizard opens. The first Chart Wizard dialog box lets you choose the type of chart you want to create. See Figure D-3. You can see a preview of the chart by clicking the Press and hold to view sample button.

3. **Click Next to accept the default chart type of column**
   The second dialog box lets you choose the data being charted and whether the series are in rows or columns. Currently, the rows are selected as the data series. You could switch this by clicking the Columns radio button located under the Data range. Since you selected the data before clicking the Chart Wizard button, the correct range A5:G10 displays in the Data range text box. Satisfied with the selections, you accept the default choices.

4. **Click Next**
   The third Chart Wizard dialog box shows a sample chart using the data you selected. Notice that the regions (the rows in the selected range) are plotted according to the months (the columns in the selected range), and that the months were added as labels for each data series. Notice also that there is a legend showing each region and its corresponding color on the chart. Here, you can choose to keep the legend, add a chart title, and add axis titles. You add a title.

5. **Click the Chart title text box, then type Nomad Ltd Regional Sales**
   After a moment, the title appears in the Sample Chart box. See Figure D-4.

6. **Click Next**
   In the last Chart Wizard dialog box, you determine the location of the chart. A chart can be displayed on the same sheet as the data, or a separate sheet in the workbook. You decide to display the chart on the current sheet.

Trouble?

If you want to delete a chart, select it then press [Delete].

7. **Click Finish**
   The column chart appears, as shown in Figure D-5. Your chart might look slightly different. Just as you had hoped, the chart shows the dramatic increase in sales between May and June. The **selection handles**, the small squares at the corners and sides of the chart borders, indicate that the chart is selected. Anytime a chart is selected (as it is now), the Chart toolbar appears. It might be floating, as shown in Figure D-5, or it might be fixed at the top or bottom of the worksheet window.

FIGURE D-3: First Chart Wizard dialog box

Chart types   Chart sub-types

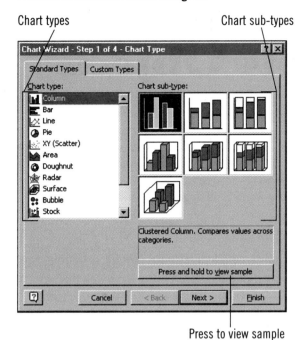

Press to view sample

FIGURE D-4: Third Chart Wizard dialog box

Sample chart   Title added   Legend

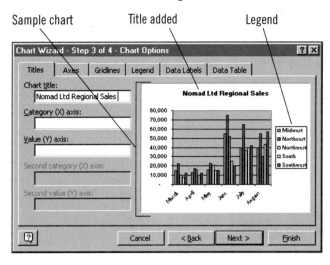

FIGURE D-5: Worksheet with column chart

Floating chart toolbar   Title   Legend

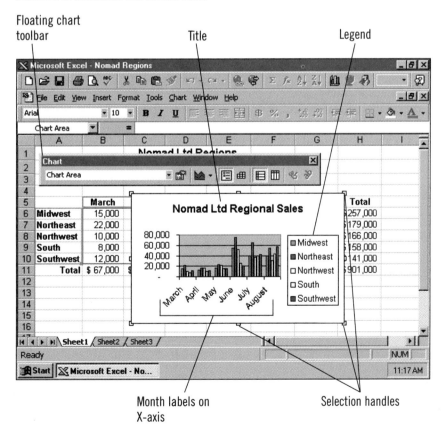

Month labels on X-axis   Selection handles

Excel 97

Moving and Resizing a Chart and its Objects

Charts are graphics, or drawn **objects**, and have no specific cell or range address. You can move charts anywhere on a worksheet without affecting formulas or data in the worksheet. You can even put them on another sheet. You can also easily resize a chart to improve its appearance by dragging the selection handles. Drawn objects such as charts can contain other objects that you can move and resize. To move an object, select it then drag it or cut and copy it to a new location. To resize an object, use the selection handles. ◄───── Evan wants to increase the size of the chart and position it below the worksheet data. He also wants to change the position of the legend.

1. Make sure the chart is still selected. Scroll the worksheet until **row 28** is visible, then position the pointer over the white space around the chart
   The pointer shape ⬚ indicates that you can move the chart or use a selection handle to resize it.

Trouble?

If the Chart toolbar is in the way of the legend, move it out of your way first.

2. Press and hold the mouse button and drag the chart until the lower edge of the chart is in **row 28** and the left edge of the chart is in **column A**, then release the mouse button
   A dotted outline of the chart perimeter appears as the chart is being moved, the pointer changes to ✛, and the chart moves to the new location.

3. Position the pointer over one of the selection handles on the right border until it changes to ↔, then drag the right edge of the chart to the **middle of column I**
   The chart is widened. See Figure D-6.

4. Position the pointer over the top middle selection handle until it changes to ↕, then drag it to the **top of row 12**
   Now, you move the legend up so that it is slightly lower than the chart title.

5. Click the **legend** to select it, then drag it to the upper-right corner of the chart until it is slightly lower than the chart title
   Selection handles appear around the legend when you click it, and a dotted outline of the legend perimeter appears as you drag.

6. Press [Esc] to deselect the legend. The legend is now repositioned. See Figure D-7.

7. Save your work

FIGURE D-6: Worksheet with reposition and resized chart

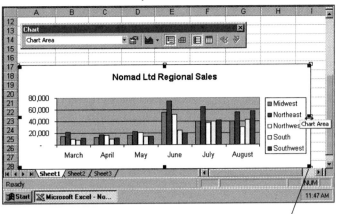

Widened to column I

FIGURE D-7: Worksheet with repositioned legend

Chart menu   Repositioned legend

Viewing multiple worksheets

A workbook can be organized with a chart on one sheet and the data on another sheet. With this organization, you can still see the data next to the chart by opening multiple windows of the same workbook. This allows you to see portions of multiple sheets at the same time. Click Window on the menu bar, then click New Window. A new window containing the current workbook opens. To see the windows next to each other, click Window on the menu bar, click Arrange, then choose one of the options in the Arrange Windows dialog box. You can open one worksheet in one window and a different worksheet in the second window. See Figure D-8. To close one window without closing the worksheet, double-click the control menu box on the window you want to close.

FIGURE D-8: Workbook with two windows open

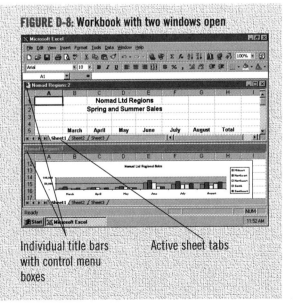

Individual title bars   Active sheet tabs
with control menu
boxes

Editing a Chart

Once you've created a chart, it's easy to modify it. You can change data values in the worksheet, and the chart will automatically be updated to reflect the new data. You can also easily change chart types using the buttons on the Chart toolbar. Table D-2 shows and describes the Chart toolbar buttons. ✐ Evan looks over his worksheet and realizes he entered the wrong data for the Northwest region in July and August. After he corrects this data, he wants to find out what percentage of total sales the month of June represents. He will convert the column chart to a pie chart to find this out.

Steps 1 2 3 4

1. **Scroll the worksheet so that you can see both the chart and row 8, containing the Northwest region's sales figures, at the same time**
   As you enter the correct values, watch the columns for July and August in the chart change.

2. **Click cell F8, type 49000 to correct the July sales figure, press [→], type 45000 in cell G8, then press [Enter]**
   The Northwest columns for July and August reflect the increased sales figures. See Figure D-9.

3. **Select the chart by clicking anywhere within the chart border, then click the Chart Type list arrow ▨ ▾ on the Chart toolbar**
   The chart type buttons appear, as shown in Figure D-10.

4. **Click the 2-D Pie Chart button ◕**
   The column chart changes to a pie chart showing total sales by month (the columns in the selected range). See Figure D-11. (You may need to scroll up to see the chart.) You look at the pie chart, takes some notes, and then decide to convert it back to a column chart. You now want to see if the large increase in sales would be better presented with a three-dimensional column chart.

5. **Click ▨ ▾, then click the 3-D Column Chart button ▦ to change the chart type**
   A three-dimensional column chart appears. You note that the three-dimensional column format is too crowded, so you switch back to the two-dimensional format.

Time To

✔ Save

6. **Click ▦ ▾, then click the 2-D Column Chart button ▥ to change the chart type**

TABLE D-2: **Chart Type buttons**

button	description	button	description
▨	Displays 2-D area chart	▨	Displays 3-D area chart
▤	Displays 2-D bar chart	▤	Displays 3-D bar chart
▥	Displays 2-D column chart	▦	Displays 3-D column chart
▨	Displays 2-D line chart	✖	Displays 3-D line chart
◕	Displays 2-D pie chart	◓	Displays 3-D pie chart
▨	Displays 2-D scatter chart	▨	Displays 3-D surface chart
◉	Displays 2-D doughnut chart	▯	Displays 3-D cylinder chart
✦	Displays radar chart	▲	Displays 3-D cone chart

FIGURE D-9: Worksheet with new data entered for the Northwest region

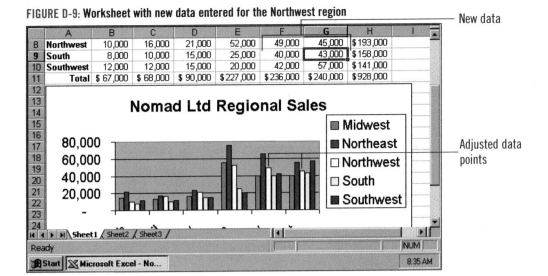

New data

Adjusted data points

FIGURE D-10: Chart Type list box

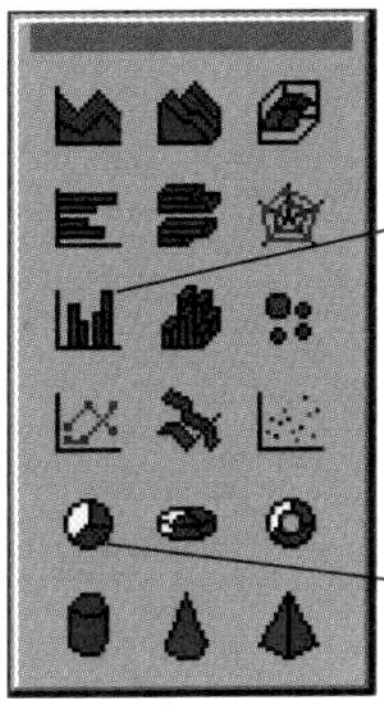

2-D Column Chart icon

2-D Pie Chart icon

FIGURE D-11: Pie chart

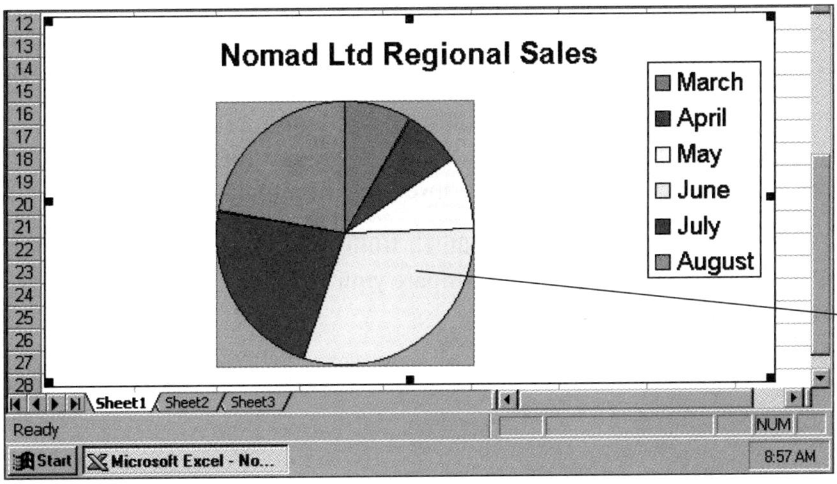

June sales pie slice

Rotating a chart

In a three-dimensional chart, columns or bars can sometimes be obscured by other data series within the same chart. You can rotate the chart until a better view is obtained. Double-click the chart, click the tip of one of its axes, then drag the handles until a more pleasing view of the data series appears. See Figure D-12.

FIGURE D-12: 3-D chart rotated with improved view of data series

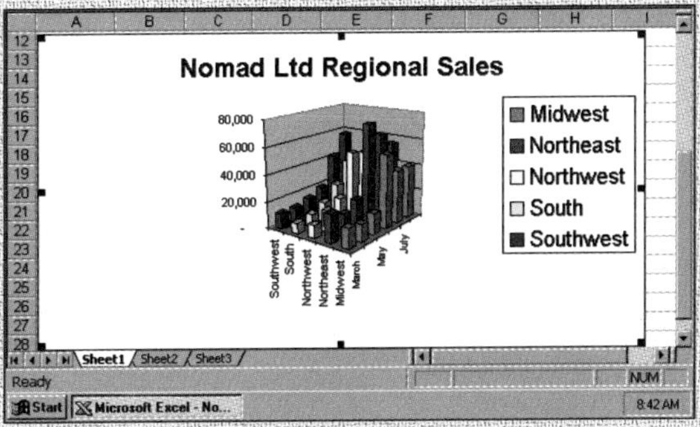

Changing the Appearance of a Chart

After you've created a chart using the Chart Wizard, you can modify its appearance by changing the colors of data series and adding or eliminating a legend and gridlines using the Chart toolbar and the Chart menu. Gridlines are the horizontal lines in the chart that enable the eye to follow the value on an axis. The corresponding Chart toolbar buttons are listed in Table D-3.

Evan wants to make some changes in the appearance of his chart. He wants to see if the chart looks better without gridlines, and he wants to change the color of a data series.

Steps

→

1. Make sure the chart is still selected
You want to see how the chart looks without gridlines. Gridlines currently appear on the chart.

2. Click Chart on the menu bar, then click Chart Options

3. Click the Gridlines tab in the Chart Options dialog box, then click the Major Gridlines checkbox for the Value (Y) Axis to remove the check and deselect this option
The gridlines disappear from the sample chart in the dialog box, as shown in Figure D-13. You decide that the gridlines are necessary to the chart's readability.

4. Click the Major Gridlines checkbox for the Value (Y) Axis, then click OK
The gridlines reappear. You are not happy with the color of the columns for the South data series and would like the columns to stand out more.

5. With the chart selected, double-click any column in the South data series
Handles appear on all the columns in the South data series, and the Format Data Series dialog box opens, as shown in Figure D-14. Make sure the Patterns tab is the front-most tab.

6. Click the dark green box (in the third row, fourth from the left), then click OK
All the columns in the series are dark green. Compare your finished chart to Figure D-15. You are pleased with the change.

7. Save your work

TABLE D-3: **Chart enhancement buttons**

button	use	button	use
	Displays formatting dialog box for the selected chart element		Charts data by row
	Selects chart type		Charts data by column
	Adds/Deletes legend		Angles selected text downward
	Creates a data table within the chart		Angles selected text upward

FIGURE D-13: **Chart Options dialog box**

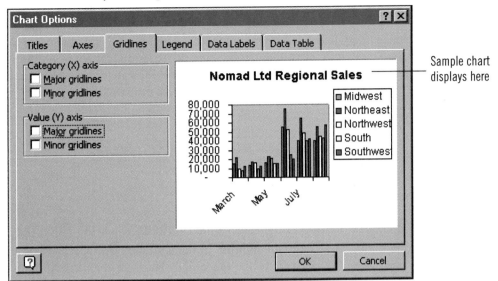

Sample chart
displays here

FIGURE D-14: **Format Data Series dialog box**

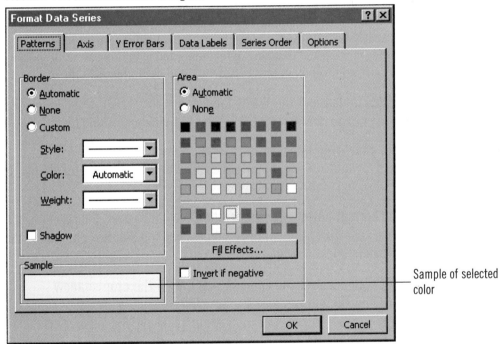

Sample of selected
color

FIGURE D-15: **Chart with formatted data series**

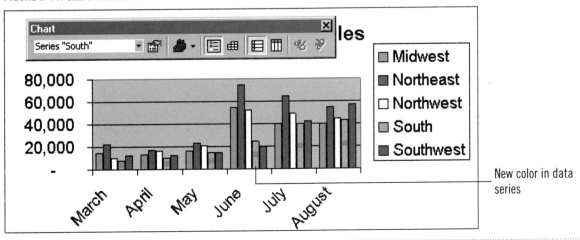

New color in data
series

Excel 97

Enhancing a Chart

There are many ways to enhance a chart to make it easier to read and understand. You can create titles for the X-axis and Y-axis, add graphics, or add background color. You can even format the text you use in a chart. ✐▬▬▬ Evan wants to improve the appearance of his chart by creating titles for the X-axis and Y-axis. He also decides to add a drop shadow to the title.

1. **Make sure the chart is selected**
   You want to add descriptive text to the X-axis.

2. **Click Chart on the menu bar, click Chart Options, click the Titles tab in the Chart Options dialog box, then type Months in the Category (X) Axis text box**
   The word "Months" appears below the month labels in the sample chart, as shown in Figure D-16. You now add text to the Y-axis.

3. **Click the Value (Y) Axis text box, type Sales, then click OK**
   A selected text box containing "Sales" appears to the left of the Y-axis. Once the Chart Options dialog box is closed, you can move the axis title to a new position, by clicking on an edge of the selection and dragging it. If you wanted to edit the axis title, position the pointer over the selected text box until it becomes Ⅰ and click, then edit the text.

4. **Press [Esc] to deselect the Y-axis label**
   Next you decide to draw a rectangle with a drop shadow around the title.

5. **Click the chart title to select it**
   If necessary, you may have to move the Chart toolbar. You use the Format button on the Chart toolbar to create a drop shadow.

6. **Click the Format button 🖼 on the Chart toolbar to open the Format Chart Title dialog box, make sure the Patterns tab is active, click the Shadow checkbox, then click OK**
   A drop shadow appears around the title.

7. **Press [Esc] to deselect the chart title and view the drop shadow**
   Compare your chart to Figure D-17.

8. **Save your work**

QuickTip

The Format button 🖼 opens a dialog box with the appropriate formatting options for the selected chart element.

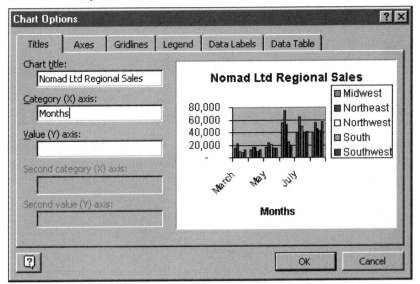

FIGURE D-17: Enhanced chart

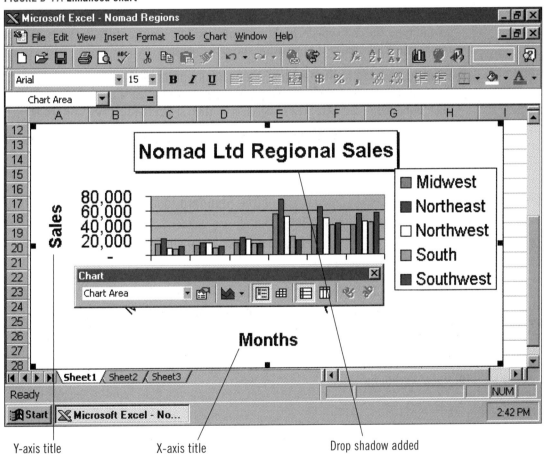

Y-axis title   X-axis title   Drop shadow added

Changing text font and alignment in charts

The font and the alignment of axis text can be modified to make it more readable or to better fit within the plot area. With a chart selected, double-click the text to be modified. The Format Axis dialog box appears. Click the Font or the Alignment tab, make the desired changes, then click OK.

Adding Text Annotations and Arrows to a Chart

You can add arrows and text annotations to highlight information in your charts. Text annotations are labels that you add to a chart to draw attention to a certain part of it. ✏️ Evan wants to add a text annotation and an arrow to highlight the June sales increase.

1. Make sure the chart is selected

You want to call attention to the June sales increase by drawing an arrow that points to the top of the June data series with the annotation, "After advertising campaign." To enter the text for an annotation, you simply start typing.

2. Type After advertising campaign then click the Enter button ✔ on the formula bar

As you type, the text appears in the formula bar. After you confirm the entry, the text appears in a floating selected text box within the chart window.

3. Point to an edge of the text box, then press and hold the left mouse button

The pointer should be ✛. If the pointer changes to ⌶ or ↔, release the mouse button, click outside the text box area to deselect it, then select the text box and repeat Step 3.

4. Drag the text box above the chart, as shown in Figure D-18, then release the mouse button

You are ready to add an arrow.

5. Click the Drawing button 🖉 on the Standard toolbar

The Drawing toolbar appears.

6. Click the Arrow button ↘ on the Drawing toolbar

The pointer changes to +.

QuickTip

You can also insert text and an arrow in the data section of a worksheet by clicking the Text Box button 🖻 on the Drawing toolbar, drawing a text box, typing the text, and then adding the arrow.

7. Position + under the word "advertising" in the text box, click the left mouse button, drag the line to the June sales, then release the mouse button

An arrowhead appears pointing to the June sales. Compare your finished chart to Figure D-19.

8. Click the Drawing button 🖉 to close the Drawing toolbar

9. Save your work

FIGURE D-18: **Repositioning text annotation**

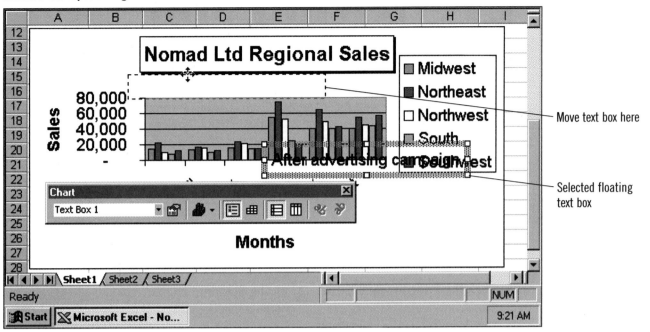

Move text box here

Selected floating text box

FIGURE D-19: **Completed chart with text annotation and arrow**

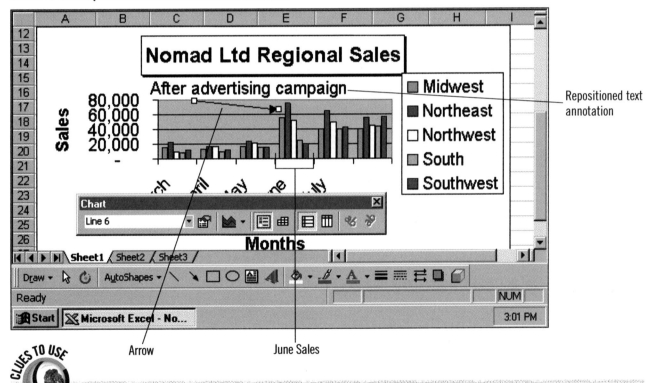

Repositioned text annotation

Arrow

June Sales

Pulling out a pie slice

Just as an arrow can call attention to a data series, you can emphasize a pie slice by exploding it, or pulling it away from, the pie chart. Once the chart is in Edit mode, click the pie to select it, click the desired slice to select only that slice, then drag the slice away from the pie, as shown in Figure D-20.

FIGURE D-20: **Exploded pie slice**

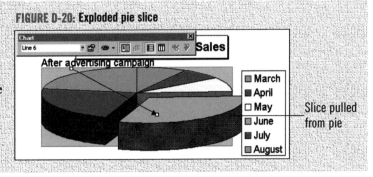

Slice pulled from pie

Previewing and Printing a Chart

After you complete a chart to your satisfaction, you will need to print it. You can print a chart by itself, or as part of the worksheet. ━━━ Evan is satisfied with the chart and wants to print it for the annual meeting. He will print the worksheet and the chart together, so that the shareholders can see the actual sales numbers for each tour type.

Steps

1. Press [Esc] twice to deselect the arrow and the chart
If you wanted to print only the chart without the data, you would leave the chart selected.

2. Click the Print Preview button 🔍 **on the Standard toolbar**
The Print Preview window opens. You decide that the chart and data would look better if they were printed in landscape orientation—that is, with the page turned sideways. To change the orientation of the page, you must alter the page setup.

3. Click the Setup button to display the Page Setup dialog box, then click the Page tab

4. Click the Landscape radio button in the Orientation section
See Figure D-21.
Because each page has a left default margin of 0.75", the chart and data will print too far over to the left of the page. You change this using the Margins tab.

5. Click the Margins tab, click the Horizontal checkbox in the Center on Page section, then click OK
The print preview of the worksheet appears again. The data and chart are centered on the page that has a landscape orientation, and no gridlines appear. See Figure D-22. You are satisfied with the way it looks and print it.

6. Click Print to display the Print dialog box, then click OK
Your printed report should look like the image displayed in the Print Preview window.

7. Save your work

8. Close the workbook and exit Excel

FIGURE D-21: **Page tab of the Page Setup dialog box**

Landscape selected

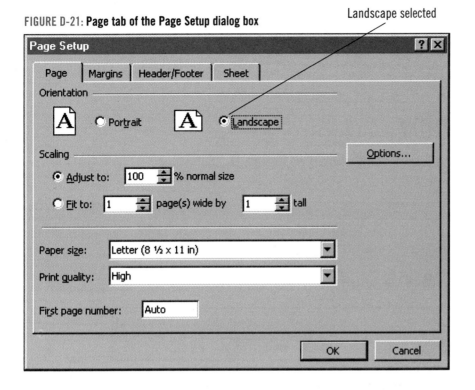

FIGURE D-22: **Chart and data ready to print**

Orientation changed
to landscape

Centered on page

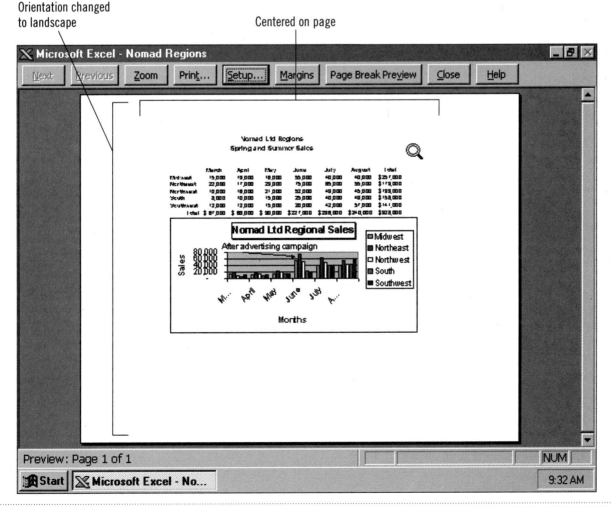

Practice

▶ Concepts Review

Label each of the elements of the Excel chart shown in Figure D-23.

FIGURE D-23

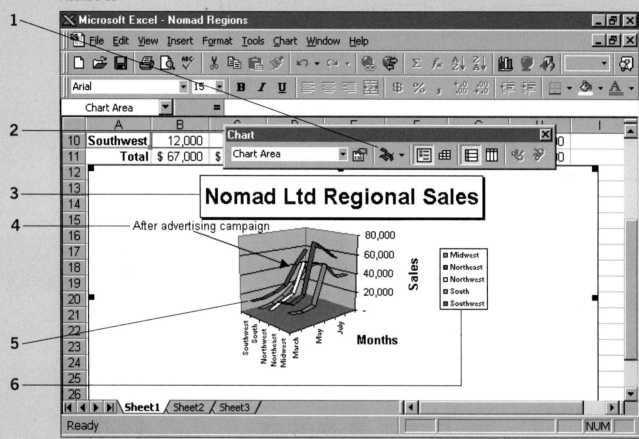

Match each of the statements with its chart type.

7. Column *e*

8. Area *a*

9. Pie *b*

10. Combination *c*

11. Line *d*

a. Shows how volume changes over time

b. Compares data as parts of a whole

c. Displays a column and line chart using different scales of measurement

d. Compares trends over even time intervals

e. Compares data over time—the Excel default

Select the best answer from the list of choices.

12. The box that identifies patterns used for each data series is a
   a. Data point   **b.** Plot   **c.** Legend   **d.** Range

13. What is the term for a row or column on a chart?
   a. Range address   **b.** Axis title   **c.** Chart orientation   **d.** Data series

► Skills Review

1. Create a worksheet and plan a chart.
   a. Start Excel, open a new workbook, then save it as Software Used to your Student Disk.
   b. Enter the information from Table D-4 in your worksheet in range A1:E6. Resize columns and rows.
   c. Save your work.
   d. Sketch a chart for a two-dimensional column chart that shows software distribution by department.

TABLE D-4

	Excel	Word	WordPerfect	PageMaker
Accounting	10	1	9	0
Marketing	2	9	0	6
Engineering	12	5	7	1
Personnel	2	2	2	1
Production	6	3	4	0

2. Create a chart.
   a. Select the range you want to chart.
   b. Click the Chart Wizard button.
   c. Complete the Chart Wizard dialog boxes and build a two-dimensional column chart on the same sheet as the data, having a different color bar for each department and with the title "Software Distribution by Department."
   d. Save your work.

3. Move and resize a chart and its objects.
   a. Make sure the chart is still selected.
   b. Move the chart beneath the data.
   c. Drag the chart's selection handles so it fills the range A7:G22.
   d. Click the legend to select it.
   e. Make the legend longer by about ½".
   f. Change the placement of the legend to the bottom right corner of the chart area.
   g. Save your work.

4. Edit a chart.
   a. Change the value in cell B3 to 6.
   b. Click the chart to select it.
   c. Click the Chart Type list arrow on the Chart toolbar.
   d. Click the 3-D Column Chart button in the list.
   e. Rotate the chart to move the data.
   f. Save your work.

5. Change the appearance of a chart.
   a. Change the chart type to 2-D column chart.
   b. Make sure the chart is still selected.
   c. Turn off the displayed gridlines.
   d. Change the X- and Y-axis font to Times New Roman.
   e. Turn the gridlines back on.
   f. Save your work.

6. Enhance a chart.
   a. Make sure the chart is still selected, then click Chart on the menu bar, click Chart Options, then click the Titles tab.
   b. Click the Category (X) axis text box and type "Department."
   c. Click the Value (Y) axis text box, type "Types of Software," and then click OK.
   d. Change the size of the X and Y axes font and the legend font to 8 pt.
   e. Save your work.

7. Adding a text annotation and arrows to a chart.
   a. Select the chart.
   b. Create the text annotation "Need More Computers."
   c. Drag the text annotation about one inch above any of the Personnel bars.
   d. Change the font size of the annotation text to 8 pt.
   e. Click the Arrow button on the Drawing toolbar.
   f. Click below the text annotation, drag down any one of the Personnel bars, then release the mouse button.
   g. Open a second window so you can display the data in the new window and the chart in the original window.
   h. Close the second window.
   i. Save your work.

8. Preview and print a chart.
   a. Deselect the chart, then click the Print Preview button on the Standard toolbar.
   b. Center the data and chart on the page and change the paper orientation to landscape.
   c. Click Print in the Print Preview window.
   d. Save your work, close the workbook, then exit Excel.

► Independent Challenges

1. You are the operations manager for the Springfield Recycling Center. The Marketing Department wants you to create charts for a brochure to advertise a new curbside recycling program. The data provided contains percentages of collected recycled goods. You need to create charts that show:

- How much of each type of recycled material Springfield collected in 1995 and what percentage each type represents. The center collects paper, plastics, and glass from business and residential customers.
- The yearly increases in the total amounts of recycled materials the center has collected since its inception three years ago. Springfield has experienced a 30% annual increase in collections.

To complete this independent challenge:

1. Prepare a worksheet plan that states your goal and identifies the formulas for any calculations.
2. Sketch a sample worksheet on a piece of paper describing how you will create the charts. Which type of chart is best suited for the information you need to display? What kind of chart enhancements will be necessary? Will a 3-D effect make your chart easier to understand?
3. Open the workbook XL D-2 on your Student Disk, then save it as Recycling Center.
4. Add a column that calculates the 30% increase in annual collections based on the percentages given.
5. Create at least six different charts to show the distribution of the different types of recycled goods, as well as the distribution by customer type. Use the Chart Wizard to switch the way data is plotted (columns vs. rows and vice versa) and come up with additional charts.
6. After creating the charts, make the appropriate enhancements. Include chart titles, legends, and axes titles.
7. Before printing, preview the file so you know what the charts will look like. Adjust any items as needed.
8. Save your work. Print the charts, then print the entire worksheet. Close the file.
9. Submit your worksheet plan, preliminary sketches, and the final worksheet printouts.

2. One of your responsibilities at the Nuts and Bolts hardware store is to re-create the company's records using Excel. Another is to convince the current staff that Excel can make daily operations easier and more efficient. You've decided to create charts using the previous year's operating expenses. These charts will be used at the next monthly Accounting Department meeting.

Open the workbook XL D-3 on your Student Disk, and save it as Expense Charts.

To complete this independent challenge:

1. Decide which data in the worksheet should be charted. Sketch two sample charts. What type of charts are best suited for the information you need to display? What kind of chart enhancements will be necessary?
2. Create at least six different charts that show the distribution of expenses, either by quarter or expense type.
3. Add annotated text and arrows highlighting data.
4. In one chart, change the colors of the data series, and in another chart, use black-and-white patterns only.
5. Before printing, preview the file so you know what the charts will look like. Adjust any items as needed.
6. Print the charts. Save your work.
7. Submit your sketches and the final worksheet printouts.

3. The Chamber of Commerce is delighted with the way you've organized their membership roster using Excel. The Board of Directors wants to ask the city for additional advertising funds and has asked you to prepare charts that can be used in their presentation.

Open the workbook XL D-4 on your Student Disk, and save it as Chamber Charts. This file contains raw advertising data for the month of January.

To complete this independent challenge:

1. Calculate the annual advertising expenses based on the January summary data.
2. Use the raw data for January shown in the range A16:B24 to create charts.
3. Decide what types of charts would be best suited for this type of data. Sketch two sample charts. What kind of chart enhancements will be necessary?
4. Create at least four different charts that show the distribution of advertising expenses. Show January expenses and projected values in at least two of the charts.
5. Add annotated text and arrows highlighting important data. Change the colors of the data series if you wish.
6. Before printing, preview the file so you know what the charts will look like. Adjust any items as needed.
7. Print the charts. Save your work.
8. Submit your sketches and the final worksheet printouts.

4. Financial information has a greater impact on others if displayed in a chart. Using the World Wide Web you can find out current activity of stocks and create informative charts. Your company has asked you to chart current trading indexes by category.

To complete this independent challenge:

1. Open a new workbook and save it on your Student Disk as Trading Indexes.
2. Log on to the Internet and use your browser to go to http://www.course.com. From there, click the link Student On Line Companions, then click the Microsoft Office 97 Professional Edition - Illustrated: A First Course page, then click the Excel link for Unit D.
3. Use the following site to compile your data, NASDAQ [www.nasdaq.com].
4. Click the Index Activity button on the NASDAQ home page.
5. Locate Index Value data by category and retrieve this information.
6. Create a chart of the Index Values, by category.
7. Save, print, and hand in a print out of your work.

▶ Visual Workshop

Modify a worksheet using the skills you learned in this unit, using Figure D-24 for reference. Open the file XL D-5 on your Student Disk, and save it as Quarterly Advertising Budget. Create the chart, then change the data to reflect Figure D-24. Preview and print your results, and submit your printout.

FIGURE D-24

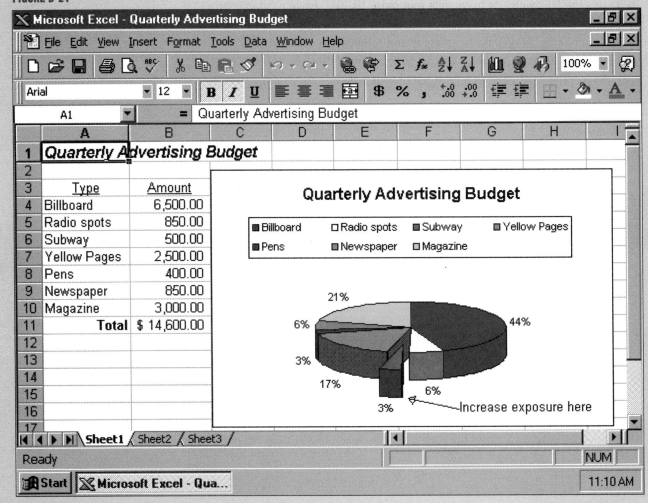

Glossary

Absolute reference A cell reference that contains a dollar sign before the column letter and/or row number to indicate the absolute, or fixed, contents of specific cells. For example, the formula A1+B1 calculates only the sum of these specific cells.

Active cell The current location of the cell pointer.

Address The location of a specific cell or range expressed by the coordinates of column and row; for example, A1.

Alignment The horizontal placement of cell contents; for example, left, center, or right.

Anchors Cells listed in a range address. For example, in the formula =SUM(A1:A15), A1 and A15 are anchors.

Area chart A line chart in which each area is given a solid color or pattern to emphasize the relationship between the pieces of charted information.

Argument A value, range of cells, or text used in a macro or function. An argument is enclosed in parentheses; for example, =SUM(A1..B1).

Arithmetic operator A symbol used in formulas, such as + or −.

Attribute The styling features such as bold, italics, and underlining that can be applied to cell contents.

AutoCalculate box The area in the status bar which displays the sum (or function of your choice) of the values in the selected range.

AutoComplete A feature that automatically completes labels entered in adjoining cells in a column.

AutoFill A feature that creates a series of text or numbers when a range is selected using the fill handle.

AutoFit Changes the width a column to accommodate its widest entry.

AutoFormat Preset schemes which can be applied to instantly format a range. Excel comes with sixteen AutoFormats which include colors, fonts, and numeric formatting.

Background color The color applied to the background of a cell.

Bar chart The bar chart displays information as the series of (horizontal) bars.

Border Edges of a selected area of a worksheet. Lines and color can be applied to borders.

Cancel button The X in the formula bar, the Cancel button removes information from the formula bar and restores the previous cell entry.

Cascading menu A subgroup of related commands that display beside a drop-down menu.

Cell The intersection of a column and row.

Cell address Unique location identified by intersecting column and row coordinates.

Cell pointer A highlighted rectangle around a cell that indicates the active cell.

Cell reference The address or name of a specific cell; cell references can be used in formulas and are relative or absolute.

Chart A graphic representation of selected worksheet information. Types include 2-D and 3-D column, bar, pie, area, and line charts.

Chart title The name assigned to a chart.

Chart Wizard A series of dialog boxes which helps create or modify a chart.

Check box A square box in a dialog box that can be clicked to turn an option on or off.

Clear A command used to erase a cell's contents, formatting, or both.

Clipboard A temporary storage area for cut or copied items that are available for pasting.

Close A command that puts a file away but keeps Excel open so that you can continue to work on other workbooks.

Column chart The default chart type in Excel. The column chart displays information as a series of (vertical) columns.

Column selector button The gray box containing the column letter above the column.

Conditional format The format of a cell is based on its value or outcome of a formula.

Confirm button The check mark in the formula bar, the Confirm button is used to confirm an entry.

Control menu box A box in the upper-left corner of a window used to resize or close a window.

Copy A command that copies the selected information and places it on the Clipboard.

Cut A command that removes the contents from a selected area of a worksheet and places them on the Clipboard.

Data marker Visible representation of a data point, such as a bar or pie slice.

Data point Individual piece of data plotted in a chart.

Data series The selected range in a worksheet that Excel converts into a graphic and displays as a chart.

Delete A command that removes cell contents from a worksheet.

Delete records A command that removes records from a list.

Dialog box A window that displays when you choose a command whose name is followed by an ellipsis (...). A dialog box allows you to make selections that determine how the command affects the selected area.

Drop-down menu A group of related commands located under a single word on the menu bar. For example, basic commands (New, Open, Save, Close, and Print) are grouped on the File menu.

Dummy column/row Blank column or row included at the end of a range which enables a formula to adjust when columns or rows are added or deleted.

Edit A change made to the contents of a cell or worksheet.

Electronic spreadsheet A computer program that performs calculations on data and organizes information. A spreadsheet is divided into columns and rows, which form individual cells.

Ellipsis A series of dots (...) indicating that more choices are available through dialog boxes.

Exploding pie slice A slice of a pie chart which has been pulled away from a pie to add emphasis.

Fill Down A command that duplicates the contents of the selected cells in the range selected below the cell pointer.

Fill handle Small square in the lower-right corner of the active cell used to copy cell contents.

Fill Right A command that duplicates the contents of the selected cells in the range selected to the right of the cell pointer.

Find A command used to locate information the user specifies.

Find & Replace A command used to find one set of criteria and replace it with new information.

Floating toolbar A toolbar within its own window; not anchored along an edge of the worksheet.

Folder A section of a disk used to store workbooks, much like a folder in a file cabinet.

Font The typeface used to display information in cells.

Format The appearance of text and numbers, including color, font, attributes, and worksheet defaults. *See also number format.*

Formula A set of instructions that you enter in a cell to perform numeric calculations (adding, multiplying, averaging, etc.); for example, +A1+B1.

Formula bar The area below the menu bar and above the Excel workspace where you enter and edit data in a worksheet cell. The formula bar becomes active when you start typing or editing cell data. The formula bar includes an Enter button and a Cancel button.

Freeze The process of making columns or rows visible.

Function A special predefined formula that provides a shortcut for commonly used calculations; for example, AVERAGE.

Gridlines Horizontal and/or vertical lines within a chart which makes the chart easier to read.

Input Information which produces desired results in a worksheet.

Insertion point Blinking I-beam which appears in the formula bar during entry and editing.

Label Descriptive text or other information that identify the rows and columns of a worksheet. Labels are not included in calculations.

Label prefix A character that identifies an entry as a label and controls the way it is displayed in the cell.

Landscape orientation Printing on a page whose dimensions are 11" (horizontally) by 8½" (vertically).

Launch To open a software program so you can use it.

Legend A key explaining the information represented by colors or patterns in a chart.

Line chart A graph of data that is mapped by a series of lines. Line charts show changes in data or categories of data over time and can be used to document trends.

Menu bar The area under the title bar on a window. The menu bar provides access to most of the application's commands.

Mode indicator A box located at the lower-left corner of the status bar that informs you of the program's status. For example, when Excel is performing a task, the work "Wait" displays.

Mouse pointer A symbol that indicates the current location of the mouse on the desktop. The mouse pointer changes shapes at times; for example, when you insert data, select a range, position a chart, change the size of a window, or select a topic in Help.

Name box The left-most area in the formula bar that shows the name or address of the area currently selected. For example, A1 refers to cell A1 of the current worksheet.

Number format A format applied to values to express numeric concepts, such as currency, date, and percent.

Object A chart or graphic image which can be moved and resized and contains handles when selected.

Office Assistant Animated help assistant that provides tips based on your work habits and lets you ask questions. The Assistant's appearance can be changed and has sounds and animation features.

Open A command that retrieves a workbook from a disk and displays it on the screen.

Order of precedence The order in which Excel calculates parts of a formula: (1) exponents, (2) multiplication and division, and (3) addition and subtraction.

Output The end result of a worksheet.

Pane A column or row which always remains visible.

Paste A command that moves information on the Clipboard to a new location. Excel pastes the formulas, rather than the result unless the Paste Special command is used.

Paste function A series of dialog boxes that lists and describes all Excel functions and assists the user in function creation.

Paste Special A command that enables you to paste formulas as values, styles, or cell contents.

Excel 97

Pie chart A circular chart that displays data as slices of pie. A pie chart is useful for showing the relationship of parts to a whole; pie slices can be extracted for emphasis.

Point A unit of measure used for fonts and row height. One inch equals 72 points.

Print Preview window A window that displays a reduced view of area to be printed.

Program Software, such as Excel or Word, that enables you to perform a certain type of task, such as data calculations or word processing.

Program Manager The main control program of Windows. All Windows applications are started from the Program Manager.

Program Menu The Windows 95 Start menu _that lists all the available programs on your computer.

Radio button A circle in a dialog box that can be clicked when only one option can be chosen.

Random Access Memory (RAM) A temporary storage area in a computer that is erased each time the computer is turned off or whenever there is a fluctuation in power. When a program is launched, it is loaded into RAM so you can work with that program.

Range A selected group of adjacent cells.

Range format A format applied to a selected range in a worksheet.

Range name A name applied to a selected range in a worksheet.

Relative cell reference Used to indicate a relative position in the worksheet. This allows you to copy and move formulas from one area to another of the same dimensions. Excel automatically changes the column and row numbers to reflect the new position.

Row height The vertical dimension of a cell.

Row selector button The gray box containing the row number to the left of the row.

Save A command used to save incremental changes to a workbook.

Save As A command used to create a duplicate of the current workbook.

Scroll bars Bars that display on the right and bottom borders of the worksheet window that give you access to information not currently visible in the current worksheet as well as others in the workbook.

Selection handles Small boxes appearing along the corners and sides of charts and graphic images which are used for moving and resizing.

Series of labels Pre-programmed series, such as days of the week and months of the year. Formed by typing the first word of the series, then dragging the fill handle to the desired cell.

Sheet A term used for worksheet.

Sheet tab Indicates the sheets contained in a workbook and their names.

Sheet tab scrolling buttons Enable you to move among sheets within a workbook.

Spell check A command that attempts to match all text in a worksheet with the words in the Excel dictionary.

Status bar Located at the bottom of the Excel window, this area lets you know information about various keys, commands, and processes.

Start To open a software program so you can use it.

Start button The rectangular button at the left end of the taskbar which displays the Windows 95 menus.

Taskbar The gray bar, usually at the bottom of the screen, containing the Start button, as well as program buttons for all programs currently running.

Text annotations Labels added to a chart to draw attention to a particular area.

Text color The color applied to the text within a cell.

Title bar The bar at the top of the window that displays the name given a workbook when it is saved and named.

Tick marks Notations of a scale of measure within a chart axis.

Toggle button A button that can be clicked to turn an option on. Clicking again turns the option off.

Tool A picture on a toolbar that represents a shortcut for performing an Excel task. For example, you can click the Save tool to save a file.

Toolbar An area within the Excel screen which contains tools. Toolbars can be docked against a worksheet edge or can float.

Values Numbers, formulas, or functions used in calculations.

What-if analysis Decision-making feature in which data is changed and automatically recalculated.

Window A framed area of a screen. Each worksheet occupies a window.

Workbook A collection of related worksheets contained within a single file.

Worksheet An electronic spreadsheet containing 256 columns by 16,384 rows.

Worksheet tab A description at the bottom of each worksheet that identified it in a workbook. In an open workbook, move to a worksheet by clicking its tab.

Worksheet window The workbook area in which data is entered.

X-axis The horizontal line in a chart.

X-axis label A label describing the x-axis of a chart.

Y-axis The vertical line in a chart.

Y-axis label A label describing the y-axis of a chart.

Zoom Enables you to focus on a larger or smaller part of the worksheet in print preview.

Excel 97

Index

Format Axis dialog box, EX D-13
Format Cells dialog box, EX C-2-3, EX C-4-5, EX C-6-7, EX C-12
Format Column commands, EX C-8
Format Data Series dialog box, EX D-11
Format Painter, EX C-3
formatting
conditional, EX C-14-15
defined, EX C-2
fonts and point sizes, EX C-4-5
values, EX C-2-3
Formatting toolbar, EX C-2, EX A-6, EX C-6-7, EX C-12
changing fonts and styles with, EX C-5
formula bar, EX B-6
formulas
with absolute cell references, copying, EX B-14-15
copying with fill handles, EX B-12-13, EX B-14
defined, EX B-6
entering in worksheets, EX B-6-7
inserting and deleting rows and columns and, EX C-10-11
order of precedence in, EX B-7
with relative cell references, copying, EX B-12-13
functions, EX B-8-9
arguments in, EX B-8
defined, EX B-8

▶G

gridlines, EX D-10
Gridlines tab, EX D-10

▶H

handles, fill, EX B-12, EX B-14
Help, EX A-14-15
highlighting attribute, EX C-6

▶I

Insert dialog box, EX C-10-11
inserting, rows and columns, EX C-10-11
insertion point, in cells, EX B-4
Italics button, on Formatting toolbar, EX C-6-7

▶L

labels
alignment of, EX C-6-7, EX A-10
attributes of, EX C-6-7
defined, EX A-10
entering in worksheets, EX A-10-11
truncated, EX A-10
landscape orientation, printing charts in, EX D-16-17
legends, for charts, EX D-3
moving, EX D-6
line charts, EX D-3
Look in list box, EX A-8

▶M

Major Gridlines checkbox, EX D-10
menu bar, EX A-6
Merge and Center button, on Formatting toolbar, EX C-6-7
Microsoft Excel program icon, EX A-4
moving
around worksheets, EX A-11
cell contents, EX B-10
charts, EX D-6-7
worksheets, EX B-16-17
multiple worksheets, viewing, EX D-7

▶N

name box, EX A-6
naming, worksheets, EX B-16-17

▶O

objects, EX D-6
Office Assistant, EX A-14-15
changing appearance of, EX A-14
closing, EX A-14
dialog box, EX A-14
online Help. See Help
Open dialog box, EX A-8, EX A-9
Operator list arrow, EX C-14
operators, arithmetic, EX B-6
order of precedence, in formulas, EX B-7
output, for worksheets, EX B-2-3

▶P

Paste function, for entering functions, EX B-8, EX B-9
Pattern list arrow, EX C-12
patterns, in worksheets, EX C-12-13
Percent Style button, on Formatting toolbar, EX C-2
pie charts, EX D-3, EX D-8
pulling slice from, EX D-15
planning, charts, EX D-2-3
pointing method, for specifying cell references in formulas, EX B-6
point size
changing, on worksheets, EX C-4-5
defined, EX C-4
precedence, order of, in formulas, EX B-7
previewing
charts, EX D-16
worksheets, EX A-12-13
Print dialog box, EX A-12-13
printing
charts, EX D-16
Help topics, EX A-14
worksheets, EX A-12-13
Print Preview
charts, EX D-16
worksheets, EX A-12
Zoom in, EX A-13

▶R

range finder, EX B-14
range names, in workbooks, EX B-5
ranges
for charts, selecting, EX D-4
defined, EX B-5, EX A-10
formatting, EX C-2
working with, EX B-4-5
recalculation, EX A-2
relative cell references
copying formulas with, EX B-12-13
defined, EX B-12
rotating, charts, EX D-9
Row Height command, EX C-9
rows
dummy, EX C-11
inserting and deleting, EX C-10-11

Index